Wording a Radiance

Wording a Radiance

Parting Conversations on God and the Church

Daniel W. Hardy

with Deborah Hardy Ford, Peter Ochs
and David F. Ford

scm press

© Daniel W. Hardy, David F. Ford, Deborah Hardy Ford and Peter Ochs

Published in 2010 by SCM Press
Editorial office
13–17 Long Lane,
London, EC1A 9PN, UK

SCM Press is an imprint of Hymns Ancient and Modern Ltd
(a registered charity)
13A Hellesdon Park Road
Norwich NR6 5DR

www.scm-canterburypress.co.uk

British Library Cataloguing in Publication data

A catalogue record for this book is available
from the British Library

978-0-334-04208-2

Typeset by Regent Typesetting, London
Printed and bound by
CPI Antony Rowe, Chippenham SN14 6LH

Contents

Part Four

For Perrin, Dan, Jen and Chris

'Some love is mine,

And always mine. A peace. A radiance
I've wanted to word but can't . . .'

(Micheal O'Siadhail)

'I've been content ever since the onset of this cancer to be drawn into death, but I don't take this negatively at all: it is also being drawn into life and the two are closely tied together . . . I don't know how: being drawn into death is also being drawn into life . . . Perhaps I am being a sort of sign of attraction, going ahead of you into the mystery, an attraction not into anything clear and unambiguous but into a light that is the mystery of death and life, and therein God.'

'These things are to do with fundamental impulses in me: to go deeper and deeper into things, for myself and with others; but it is more than that, it's how you reach into that to find greater depths which are found again to be the depths of God. This is about my almost insatiable *concern* for God, not just for knowledge about God but a more insatiable thirst again than that . . .'

'. . . it is a question of allowing the divine to flood in without inhibition. I can't get away from the fact that a lot more is to be said about how things and people are knit together in the divine abundance – an indefinite resource of human wholeness, and wholeness for the universe too. What is it that people are growing into? There is a far more profound human integrity than we have yet glimpsed. What is it that grows a good, whole human being and a good society?'

(Daniel W. Hardy in conversation, September – November 2007)

Preface

Farewell, farewell! But this I tell
To thee, thou Wedding-Guest!
He prayeth well, who loveth well
Both man and bird and beast.

He prayeth best, who loveth best
All things both great and small;
For the dear God who loveth us,
He made and loveth all.

(Samuel Taylor Coleridge, *Rime of the Ancient Mariner*)

In one of his last published works, an essay on Coleridge's *Opus Maximum*, Daniel W. Hardy reflects on the dynamic of love in these few (his favourite) verses: 'The scope . . . widens from all that is animate . . . to include everything'; 'the intensity of love increases from "well" to "best,"'; correlatively, the intensity of prayer increases from 'well' to 'best'; and 'the greatest intensity of prayer (relationship to God) becomes actual not because of human capacity but because God made and loves both us. . . . and all things . . . (accordingly) prayer includes not only loving attentiveness but also the reasoning of that which is made by God'.

The last six months of his life had that quality of intensity: the unprecedented element in which was his experience of being drawn deeper into God's light and love while on pilgrimage in the Holy Land.

This book draws on three series of conversations, which he sustained during those months with his co-authors: Peter Ochs, his friend; Deborah Ford, his daughter; and David Ford, his son-in-law. Of course there were many others too. It tells the story of his experiences on pilgrimage to the Holy Land just weeks before the diagnosis of an aggressive brain tumour; of his coming to terms with those experiences and his approaching death.

Daniel took this time very seriously and dropped many of the activities and commitments that previously took up his time and energy. There were painful decisions about whom to meet with (giving priority to family, graduate students and a few friends, with whom he was used to having sustained conversation); and one of the most agonizing decisions was to give up on the hope of writing a book on the Church he had contracted with Cambridge University Press, which during its long gestation (going back around 20 years to his time in Durham) had become a lens through which he thought about the whole of theology and society.

Yet the decision was made immeasurably easier by the offer of Peter Ochs to be his interlocutor and scribe for a book that would try to distil the key themes and thought of his ecclesiology, together with the understanding that those regular conversations with Peter would be edited with others into the present volume. Daniel showed massive, deliberate determination in giving high priority to these times and he was able to dictate Chapters 2 to 5 of this book, giving something of what would have been the main thrust of that monograph. The pilgrimage added surprising elements to it, as did his terminal illness. So this book was conceived directly in conversation with him, and he was deeply encouraged to know it would happen.

The problem with the density of the material for this book is that it has been quite a challenge to articulate it in digestible form. It is divided into four sections: Part 1 (Chapter 1) begins with 'A Portrait of My Father' by Deborah Hardy Ford and then moves into Daniel's own voice and the story of his pilgrimage as he told it to her. (Different 'versions' of this narrative – as told distinctively to each of the three authors – continue to re-emerge throughout the book.) Part 2 is transcribed and edited by Peter Ochs. Each chapter (2–5) recollects and then reflects theologically on key moments and places during the pilgrimage for Daniel: from the headwaters of the Jordan; to Jericho; to St George's Cathedral in Jerusalem; and walking through the tunnel under the Temple Mount. In Part 3 (Chapter 6, 'Living Theology in the Face of Death'), David Ford meditates on the impact of Daniel's thinking in this book, measured through their conversations both over years of rich collegiality (right back to those culminating in their book *Jubilate* in 1984) and through the intensification of their last six months. The book closes with Part 4 (Chapter 7, written and edited by Deborah Ford) and Daniel's 'Farewell Discourses': conversations he had with Deborah about his own death and dying in the last weeks and days of his life. There is also an appendix containing a selected bibliography of Daniel's writings.

It has been an astonishing privilege to be caught up in the spirit and movement of this work. We are indebted to many people in helping this book to come about: first and foremost, of course, Daniel himself. Without him, it would never have begun and we have been endlessly amazed and grateful for the gift he has given: for all we learned through our conversations with him and with one other as he gradually handed it over and entrusted his book to us.

And there are many others who have generously and lovingly supported and sustained us in different ways during the months of its coming to birth: particularly Perrin, Jen, Dan and Chris (Daniel's wife and children, each of whom had profound conversations with him, but have not had the chance to voice them here); Jack, Ann and Dick (his sister and brothers); Rebecca, Rachel, Amanda, Daniel, Sarah and Matthew (his grandchildren); Vanessa and Elizabeth Ochs; Phyllis Ford; Micheal and Brid O'Siadhail; Gregory Seach; Aref Nayad; Yamina Mermer . . . It is impossible to do justice to everyone here, but we are deeply grateful to each one of them; as well as to Natalie Watson of SCM for her patience and encouragement; and to Emily Rowell for her work on the bibliography of Daniel Hardy's publications.

PART ONE

I

A Portrait of My Father
Daniel W. Hardy

9 November 1930 – 15 November 2007

Deborah Hardy Ford

... When he was at the table with them, he took bread, blessed and broke it, and gave it to them. Then their eyes were opened, and they recognized him; and he vanished from their sight. They said to each other, 'Were not our hearts burning within us while he was talking to us on the road, while he was opening the scriptures to us?'[1]

On the day when he said, 'I think I probably am dying . . .', and shortly before he stopped being able to speak, my father and I suddenly started thinking and talking about colour.[2] He described how

[t]his light I've talked about and see infused in people and between people and things isn't white light, you know. It is colour: colour in its full and wonderful range. How do *you* see colour? The colour in you and in the people you meet and how you relate to one another?[3]

And seeing as I'd never thought about it quite like that before, I had to say 'I don't know: I'll have to think about it . . .'
'What colour do you see *yourself* as?' I asked.
'Brown, I think,' he answered. 'Not too dark a brown . . . a warm, rich brown, probably with quite a lot of yellow, red, orange, and maybe some blue in it too: an earthy colour. What about *you*?'
My father never liked to talk about himself for very long: he was much more interested in looking outwards and discerning

and recognizing God in the people and world around him, in the particularities of the people and systems he was part of. Quite early on I discovered that the best way to spend time with him was to talk about God. He could never get enough of that. 'Here's all this' (as he put it). 'How is it of God?' Everything was related to God: whether it was the quantum measurement of subatomic particles or the details of Western intellectual thought or a Bach fugue or the hinge on a kitchen cabinet. It was Aquinas' *sub ratione Dei*: understanding everything in relation to God:

> I want to explore things in relation to one another: the intensity of the Lord and his presence and action in the world. Dedicated attention to the intensity of God: that's the source of theology; it's not about any academic contrivances. It has a doubling role: to explain but also to invite deeper into the mystery. It's a form of prayer done deeply within the Spirit and it requires sustained inquiry in many directions, by testing the major theologies, philosophies and sciences of modernity.

True to the colour brown, he preferred to be in the background than in the limelight ('behind the scenes'): complementing others and encouraging them to grow into the light in them in a rather hidden and underground way, creating an environment where new things could be cultivated and nurtured with the utmost patience, care and attentiveness. He was always ready and willing to encourage, praise and affirm the life and beauty deep within each person he met: captured in the spirit of this poem, written by one of his favourite poets and friends (who read another of his poems at his funeral):

Sunflower

The danger of tautening towards the sun:
To lose is to lose all.
Too much gravity and I'm undone;
If I bend, I fall.

Tell me it's all worth this venture,
Just the slightest reassurance,

And I'll open a bloom, I'll flower
At every chance.

Then praise me all the way to the sky,
Praise me with light, lover,
Oh praise me, praise me, praise me
And I live for ever.[4]

He had a remarkable gift and capacity for seeing the light and
potential in other people and situations and, somehow, to anticipate the light: to hope, believe and trust in it, and to discern and
nurture it in such a way that things and possibilities you never
dreamed were in you could come into being. He was intrigued by
'how the Divine reaches within people and forms new life within
them. How does it happen in the "inmost texture" of people?
How does it lift and transform them?'

That is what it was like when you knew that you wanted to talk
and think about *something*, but had no idea yet what that thing
might turn out to be. He could stay with you in what were often
very pregnant spaces: long, awkward, silences; waiting and not
knowing, without ever imposing himself or any of his ideas until
you were ready. But at other times, when whatever it was that
you wanted to explore with him was more developed in you, it
meant subjecting yourself to a rigorous and sometimes seemingly
relentless critique and scrutiny: that 'spirit that searches everything – even the depths of God' (1 Cor. 2.10). It was a hugely
demanding and refining process but a necessary part of getting to
the essence of whatever it was. He was never prepared (or let you
be prepared) to settle for less than the best.

It became well known within a certain Cambridge graduate
community that being put through your paces in supervision with
Professor David Ford was only a shade of things to come on the
day you were deemed ready for a meeting with Professor Dan
Hardy . . .

He was a critical judge, but one who knew what it was to be
'the judged',[5] and whatever rigour he might require you to apply
to your (or another's) thinking, he first applied it just as thor-
oughly to his own. He asked a lot of himself. As a child I often

3

wished he would be gentler and more compassionate with himself, but he did change and mellow quite a lot in latter years. He became less dogmatic, less rigid and abstract and more embodied and accepting of his own and other people's limitations: more compassionate. As well as being judge, he was also advocate, utterly on your side.

I remember an occasion when I had just passed my driving test. I was a rather unsure 17-year-old, who nevertheless thought that she was pretty clever for passing her test the first time. I slowly built up my confidence – often taking the dog with me for moral support – and gradually undertook more challenging and adventurous journeys. But the really big thing was that I was now allowed to drive not only our family estate (which I felt to be a bit of a banger), but also my father's car. He had a very beautiful and special 1930s' Mercedes, which had been passed down to him by his mother. She had shipped it all the way from America. It was shiny polished grey, with wonderful leather seats, and he was *very* proud of it. So you can imagine how chuffed I was that I was now considered trustworthy enough to drive it too. I took it out a number of times, purring through the streets; it was a dream to drive, and I loved it too. Until one day I suddenly found myself rather too close to the cars parked on either side of the road which I needed to manoeuvre through (it was quite a wide car and happened to have a left-hand drive) – it suddenly seemed a very narrow gap – and I was going too fast to be able to do anything about it. I took a deep breath in (as if that might make us smaller), but then scraped (and screeched) against the side of the car parked to my right. What made matters even worse was, when the driver of the car emerged from within, and asked me (rather surprised) what was going on . . . I soon noticed that, because his car was a Land Rover, the external knee-height 'step' accessing the passenger seat had gouged and grooved its way down the entire length of my father's car. We had come out by far the worse. The driver was surprisingly nice about it, but it's hard to describe how awful I felt: simply wretched, the shame and guilt at the consequences of my own poor judgement and recklessness, but even more so at the disappointment my father would feel at my damaging the precious car that he'd entrusted to me. I decided I had to confess immediately and drove straight (and *very* carefully) to his office. To my relief he happened to be there. He was rather surprised to see me, but when I finally blurted out the reason, he simply said, 'Well, never mind . . . We'll sort it out.' No anger, no harsh judgement, no retribution. I couldn't really believe it. And he never mentioned it again. It may seem a rather trivial example, but I can assure you it wasn't. The depth of love and mercy in his response was overwhelming.

He was humble, endlessly generous and giving of himself and his time and energy, but he was always there if you needed him – especially at the end of the day when he often worked late into the night. No matter how ordinary or insignificant something might seem to you to be bothering him with, whatever mattered to you mattered to him, and he was endlessly patient in listening to it. He never made you feel small or ignorant or stupid; he listened and attended to you in a way that raised you up to a fuller dignity and stature. He called it 'engaging people from within'. His face was gentle and kind: rich, warm brown eyes with a loving smile and light in them – that 'apple of my eye' look.

In recent years we had an ongoing conversation that went something like this: 'I'm bored, Dad: I love my work and all that I do, but intellectually I'm bored.'

'We must *do* something about that,' he said.

I had tried to talk about it with other people. but had not got very far. People had been kind and thoughtful, but somehow either too full of their own ideas of what they thought I might be interested in, or too reticent about even exploring the possibilities, unable to stay open to encouraging the as yet unrecognized raw potential or longing within. It became increasingly urgent, as he became iller and the windows of opportunity for deep conversation narrower. Until one day we finally got straight to the point (although, as was so often the case, only in response to my initiative).

'What is it that you want to think about?' my father asked.

'I'm not sure . . . That's the whole problem . . . I can't decide.'

We sat in silence together, deep calling to deep, anticipating and trusting something to emerge; some deep hope, dream or desire that I had not yet been able to recognize. 'Maybe laughter . . . or silence . . .' (We had already decided that 'remorse', on which I had already written, had had its day.) But they soon fizzled. We sat some more. (There was something very Quaker about it.) And then suddenly, from almost out of nowhere, yet also deep within myself, I knew: 'Imagining!' I said. 'That's it! That's what I want to think about for the rest of my life: not imagina*tion*, but the act of imagin*ing*.' It had happened and I was full of excitement, energy and wonder.[6]

One of the great sadnesses to me was that we had very little chance to take the conversation any further. In the months to come, my father's illness consumed him more and more, and he had to preserve whatever energy he had for what mattered most: particularly communicating the contents of this book. So it was only able to be a beginning – something that would have to be taken up and carried on with others beyond his life – and yet hugely significant in all that it had accomplished in opening up possibilities yet to come.

There was something very solid about him, but you were plunged into deep waters with him, too. He had a yearning for truth – and always (then) for fuller and deeper wisdom and truth: 'I'm always interested in everything: that's one of my problems!' His favourite summer 'book bag' – always crammed to the point of bursting – provided a wealth of reading not only for him but for the whole family, with the newest cutting-edge books on the humanities; literature; music; art; the sciences . . . He came up against the limits of language as his mind stretched and discovered new capacity and categories for the reality he was trying to do justice to; and he had endless struggles in trying to articulate, write and communicate the 'density' of what he was discovering and conceptualizing. It wasn't that he couldn't say things in plain English; I often used to say to him, 'But what do you *mean*, Dad?', and after a few minutes he could usually explain what he (or someone else) meant in perfectly simple language. But somehow, creating new words and redefining old ones was an inherent part of the ongoing expansion of his heart, mind and soul – vital to him. Language and concepts stretched him and each other into new realms, and new words and phrases came into being as he participated and went deeper into the re-creative life of the Word itself: the God who says 'I am who I am. and I shall be who I shall be,' endlessly innovative and new. My father always made you know that you were part of something much, much *bigger*.

And although I sometimes just wished that he would be satisfied with the 'good enough' and not always have to think everything through for himself (usually right from the start) once again, I grew to realize what a gift it was: to think with such freedom, openness and boldness. He was never intimidated by anything or anyone.

Some of the difficulty he had in trying to find words (he published very few of the many books he had in him) went right back. He was born in New York on 9 November 1930 into an affluent conservative American family (his European ancestors were among the earliest 'pilgrim' settlers in the USA) – the third of four children (boy, girl, boy, boy) – to 'Mr and Mrs John Alexander Hardy' (as they were always known; his mother's name was Barbara). While privileged economically, educationally and culturally, the family was perhaps less well off in other ways. Just before my father was born, his paternal grandmother died, and his parents complied with his grandfather's request that they move to live with him, so that his mother could keep house for him/them. So the family was very much under the rule and thumb of 'Grandpa', until he died in 1947 (18 years later, when they finally moved into New York City). This was an ongoing source of tension within the family, particularly with my father's parents. Another was the fact that one day shortly after the outbreak of the Second World War, and without a word to anyone, his father took himself off and signed up for the army.

They lived in a large house on a peninsula in Whitestone, a wealthy Long Island suburb, with a series of Irish nannies, so although his mother adored him, he perhaps had less of her attention than he might have (especially after the arrival of his youngest brother), and he described her as very formal and emotionally distant. The children went to the best (private) schools, but were always reminded that they were not as affluent as their peers, and were very isolated. They felt socially insecure and were never encouraged to develop friendships or to bring friends back to the house. My father remembered being very shy and how he suf-

Dan with siblings: in order from the left:
Jack (John A. Hardy Jr), Dan, Ann and Dick)

fered with a stammer throughout his childhood and adolescence:
'It was much easier to think and map than to speak.' He described
himself as speechless in some ways (even in later years), particularly in the area of emotional speech and language.

Petrol rationing during the war made it increasingly difficult
to travel back and forth to school every day, so the children were
sent off to boarding school: Dan (aged 12) and his brothers Jack
and Dick to Emerson and then on to (Phillips) Exeter Academy
(New Hampshire), and his sister Ann to Abbot Academy near
Boston (Massachusetts).

Perhaps one of the saving graces for this generation of the Hardy
family was that they found their own place of sanctuary at Twin
Lakes in the Berkshire Mountains in upstate Connecticut, where
they spent every summer. My grandfather (an engineer) designed
and built the much-loved house, which my father later went on to

own and tend for himself and which became 'home base' (in the USA) for his own family in years to come. Again, it was isolated and often lonely, but a place of great beauty, peace and the elements: a place where (as a child) he read, thought, swam, rowed, kept ducks and boats, and developed his interests in photography, film, classical music and sound systems. Church (fairly low Anglican) seems to have played some – but not a very essential – part within the life of the family as a whole during these years.

He is remembered as having quite a temper, being very stubborn at times, as frequently losing all track of time (so absorbed was he in whatever he was doing), being late for everything, as well as being fundamentally kind, responsible and sweet-natured. Even then, he was the primary care-giver of the family, tending, herding and rescuing, eager to give generously and unconditionally. He was tidy and practical, but is particularly renowned for a moment on his wedding day, when, towards the end of the reception, it suddenly became apparent that Dan was missing, only to be found some time later (much to the relief of his new wife Perrin, together with the whole party), back in his apartment, absorbed in packing for his honeymoon – oblivious of what all the fuss was about.

And my father always loved penguins, for as long as anyone can remember, especially emperor penguins.

But the lake home was also a place where he faced a lot of pain and wrestling. He suffered several prolonged and excruciating bouts of osteomyelitis[7] during his mid-teens (just before the days of penicillin); there were many summers when he was longing and yet somehow unable to write. And he was there for his last summer, too – shortly before his death, when, as well as being the place he most wanted to be, it often felt like Gethsemane.

In spite of his reluctance to talk about himself, there was one occasion when my father had no choice. Shortly before his death, he was awarded an honorary DD[8] by General Theological Seminary ('GTS' in New York City) and was invited to travel to receive it, together with giving a speech about himself, his life and his ministry.

Although there was no question of his being able to travel at this point, he was thrilled at the possibility of my being able to receive the degree and speak on his behalf; and while unable to put anything on to paper, he was still adamant that he wanted to come up with something to say. So he asked us to help him (David his colleague, friend, co-author,[9] son-in-law; and myself, his daughter, also an Anglican priest). And we spent time reflecting on his life in a way that had never been possible before: he was somehow able to say things about himself through us that he'd never been able to until then. This is the message he sent:

Dear Friends in Faith,
It is a delight and an honour to receive this honorary doctorate from General Theological Seminary and to be represented by my daughter, the Revd Deborah Ford.

The genesis of my vocation to ordination lay in my years as a student in Haverford College and in the finding of oneself before God that was encouraged and enabled by participation in its regular Quaker worship. The rhythm and pattern of worship of 'General' [Theological Seminary], (four services a day in chapel) then built on this and was the most formative thing during my time as a student here. It was a daily invitation to go deeper into the intensity of God, an attraction that has perhaps been the most fundamental dynamic of my life.

My title post (served in Christ Church, Greenwich) added a second key dynamic. This is exemplified best through my engagement with a group of young people – beginning with what really mattered and was significant for them, and then trusting, discerning and helping them to recognize the source and energy of life (God's Spirit) already at work within their lives – [and] making the deep connections with the truth of the gospel. They were hungry for this, and the group began to thrive in just a short space of time. The curacy culminated in helping to design the new daughter church of St Barnabas, strengthening an interest in architecture that in later years has proved fruitful again and again both with actual buildings and with the architectonics of theology and institutions.

I returned to GTS as a fellow and tutor for two years, accompanied by my wife Perrin, who, together with our growing family, grew to be central to my life. The experience of teaching and a sense of the crying need for theological thinking led to further study in Oxford University. Yet that was in many ways a painful disappointment, finding a theology that was too influenced by positivist philosophy and rarely confident enough to explore the depths and wonders of God and God's ways with the world.

The 21 years that followed were spent teaching in the University of Birmingham. The 'golden thread' of those rich and varied years was the pursuit of a theology that might give dedicated attention both to the intensity of God and to the way the world is, especially as described, interpreted and explained by theologians, philosophers and scientists since the sixteenth century. Exploring and testing their thought was a slow and often lonely task, but for several hours each week there was intensive conversation with the colleague who became my son-in-law, David Ford. They were wonderful hours, exploring through the lens of praise and the superabundance of God's truth and love.

Moving to the Van Mildert Professorship of Divinity in the University of Durham and a canonry in Durham Cathedral was like spiralling back to a GTS-like combination of daily worship with academic work. If I were to choose just one key element in those years it would be the fresh, multifaceted involvement in ecclesiology that has remained at the forefront of my thinking ever since.

Then I re-crossed the Atlantic to be Director of the Princeton Center of Theological Inquiry for five years. Much of my time there was spent in rethinking the Center (along lines now happily being pursued by the current Director) and in working closely with individual members from many disciplines and many countries. But judged in terms of long-term results it is probably the relationship with one member, the Jewish philosopher Peter Ochs of the University of Virginia, that has been most fruitful. He, David Ford (of Cambridge University) and I have spent much time over many years since the early 1990s working together with others to develop the practice of Scriptural Reasoning, the shared study of our scriptures by Jews, Christians and Muslims.

I was deeply gratified when GTS invited me to speak about Scriptural Reasoning during the opening conference of the

Desmond Tutu Education Center last month, and very disappointed that I could not attend for reasons of health. I am
delighted that Peter, David and others, including some Muslim
participants in Scriptural Reasoning, led two workshops (I
know that a film of this has since been broadcast on PBS [public
television]), and also that the practice had such a warm reception in the seminary. Might I take advantage of this occasion to
commend Scriptural Reasoning to you as warmly as possible? It
is one way of going deeper simultaneously into one's own faith
and into the faith of others through study and mutual mentor-
ing, and in my judgement holds considerable promise for the
twenty-first century, not least in building much-needed forms of
peaceful sociality between the Abrahamic faiths. Its fruitfulness
has most recently been seen in last week's[10] Muslim message,
A Common Word, addressed to Christian leaders, and I hope
that this seminary might be a place where that message of love
for God and neighbour is responded to wholeheartedly. If only
the Anglican Communion could learn this too! My involvement
in the 1998 Lambeth Conference and participation in some of
the Primates' meetings during the years that followed made me
long for a reconciliatory imagination and practice centred on
Scripture and nurturing a deeper and richer sociality, touching
healingly the depths of each person. May the new Desmond
Tutu Center serve this divine purpose well!

This evening's happy event brings my theological career
since its beginnings in this seminary full circle. I end with two
thoughts.

The first is on my own vocation. I see it as having been
primarily about the seeking of God's wisdom. It has been prophetic insofar as it has attempted to engage more deeply with
life in all its particularity. It has been priestly in tracing that
prophetic wisdom to its source in the divine intensity of love
and in seeking to mediate that love through the Church for the
whole world, concentratedly in the Eucharist: light and love
together. The second is a tribute to the thinker who has perhaps more than any other been my teacher and inspiration over
many decades, Samuel Taylor Coleridge. He engaged deeply
with God and most aspects of God's creation – intellectually,

imaginatively, practically, spiritually, emotionally and through much personal suffering. Above all he responded in all those ways to the attraction of the divine. He discerned the Word and the Spirit endlessly present, active and innovative, lifting the world from within, raising it into its future – giving us a huge hope in God and God's future, and inviting us intensively and unremittingly to participate in that, as we are drawn through divine love into levels of existence of which we can hardly begin to imagine or dare to dream.

In this spirit I conclude with one of the great Christian prayers, in which I invite you to join:

> For this reason I bow my knees before the Father, from whom every family in heaven and on earth takes its name. I pray that, according to the riches of his glory, he may grant that you may be strengthened in your inner being with power through his Spirit, and that Christ may dwell in your hearts through faith, as you are being rooted and grounded in love. I pray that you may have the power to comprehend, with all the saints, what is the breadth and length and height and depth, and to know the love of Christ that surpasses knowledge, so that you may be filled with all the fullness of God. Now to him who by the power at work within us is able to accomplish abundantly far more than all we can ask or imagine, to him be glory in the church and in Christ Jesus to all generations, for ever and ever. Amen.[11]

(Daniel W. Hardy, 18 October 2007)

On that same day when we talked about colour and my father said, 'I think I probably am dying,' I asked, 'Are you ready, then?'

He answered peacefully, 'Yes, I think I am, I think I am ready to just slip away. My main concern is the unfinished business: mostly this book. It's not the shape I first imagined it would be.'

'Is there still much to do?' I asked. 'It sounds like you've already come a long way.'

'It's indeterminate,' was his reply. And of course he was suddenly speaking about the pain of recognizing all he had to let go of, too: particularly his beloved friend, Peter. This was the closest he ever got to acknowledging some of his own pain and loss in his dying. I empathized, but told him that the process of this book had been amazing to me. It seemed even more appropriate, some-how, that it would have to be continued and finished in the presence of his absence. It had a life of its own, which was bigger than him, and, as he handed it over and entrusted it to us, it would draw us and others up into its life and energy even after his death. As we worked on it, he would be right there in our midst (and he has been): and we went on to speak of the dynamic of the Trinity and of the Eucharist – gathering everything up and together in its life and truth.

Peter describes him as

a pastor's pastor – seeing light in the other, light as attractiveness in and with the other. He is a pastor of others within the Eucharist; within the Anglican Communion, pastor on behalf of Abrahamic communions and to human communities more generally, all of whom he sees lit up by the divine attractiveness itself: the great cosmic and ecclesial and divine communion of lights which draws him to it and to us and draws us to be near him.

The actual genesis of the writing of this book was when the three of us (Peter, David and I) gathered in the room (at home) where he had breathed his last just a few days earlier: gathered to simply be together and to pray and keep watch over his body before his burial the following day.

We had decided to open our scriptures together, 'Scriptural Reasoning-style'[12] (something that mattered hugely to my father and in which he 'found' himself most fully in recent years[13]): the founding fathers of SR and (because one father was now dead), a daughter, too. Peter turned to a psalm in his prayer book to be read by Jewish mourners after the death of a loved one, so we decided to make that our text.

It was a profound time and is impossible to recapture adequately here, but as we honoured the life of this beloved father and friend together and tried to make some sense of his life and death in the midst of our grief, something amazing happened as the Word came alive and our hearts 'burned within us'.

Psalm 42

כאיל תערג על אפיקי מים כן נפשי תערג אליך
אלהים:
צמאה נפשי לאלהים לאל חי מתי אבוא ואראה
פני אלהים:

As a deer longs for flowing streams,
so my soul longs for you, O God.
My soul thirsts for God, for the living God:
when shall I come and behold the face of God? (vv. 1–3)

In the shock of our grief, we had forgotten that this psalm had
been so much at the heart of my father's pilgrimage in the Holy
Land: itself a psalm of pilgrimage, and somehow able to draw
all our pilgrimages into one. He described his longing for God at
the headwaters of the Jordan[14] as 'my almost insatiable concern
for God, not just for knowledge of God but a more insatiable
thirst again than that': the intensification of a lifetime's prompt-
ing, the mystery of going deeper into God, the 'living water', who,
in the very process of satisfying, creates the thirst and desire for
more. It was our prayer too. It echoed our longing and need to
know God amid the barrenness of our loss, and there were also
echoes (for me, at least) of 'For now we see in a mirror, dimly,
but then we shall see face to face. Now I know only in part; then I
will know fully, even as I have been fully known' (1 Cor. 13.12).
This was the beginning of orienting ourselves to a new place and
way of seeing and experiencing things; my father had passed over
a threshold where we could not yet go: 'Where I am going you
cannot come . . . I give you a new commandment . . .' (Jesus to his
disciples, John 13.33–34).

היתה לי דמעתי לחם יומם ולילה באמר אלי
כל היום איה אלהיך:

My tears have been my food day and night,
while they say to me all day long,
'Where is your God?' (v. 3)

Although at first it was difficult for us to get a sense of this in relation to my father's life, as we sat and listened to the psalm in my father's voice, we began to be honest about some of the difficult and darker strands of his life: particularly the Oxford years, of which he wrote:

> If I had wanted some trials by which to refine my calling, they were there all right. At the time, Oxford philosophy – and such was its influence, much else besides – was largely in the grip of logical positivism, a movement that reduced Christian belief either to nonsense or simple moral guidance . . . It was not a comfortable time, not least because no one, certainly not those with whom I worked, had very helpful ideas of the way forward. It was good because intensive study day after day developed my capacity for concentrated thought, but the options open to theologians like me were very limited, and it was a deeply frustrating time.[15]

More recently, he referred to this experience as a 'black hole' (his words) and began to speak more openly of the experience of having his doctoral thesis rejected and his agony and shame in feeling completely misheard and misunderstood: 'a misfit'. He was offered an MPhil instead and refused to accept it, and for years there was a lingering sense of bitterness in him in relation to it. The years at the Center of Theological Inquiry in Princeton had their difficulties, too:[16]

> Those were interesting years, gathering the best scholars and helping them work together, while also establishing regular consultations, bringing together leading specialists from around the world to meet regularly to address special topics, but the tensions with the seminary and the politics of the time inhibited the potential there and when it became evident that I had brought the place as far as I could without further assistance, and none was forthcoming, it seemed right to retire from there and get back to work.

אלה אזכרה ואשפכה עלי נפשי כי אעבר בסך
אדדם עד בית אלהים בקול רנה ותודה המון
חוגג:

> These things I remember as I pour out my soul:
> how I went with the procession
> and led them to the house of God,
> with joyous songs of thanksgiving:
> a festive multitude. (v. 4)

And yet we remembered how (as for the psalmist), no matter what he might be going through, regular, faithful worship was always such a priority for him.[17] The deeply formative rhythms of prayer and worship established through his years at school, college and seminary, with their daily dynamic of reorientation to God, were continued through his involvement in a series of local churches. He was committed to the daily discipline and nurture of the ordinary things as well as the highbrow. Preaching, pastoring and regular participation in celebrating the Eucharist were essential to his vocation; so, at times when his jobs were in more secular settings, he was careful to develop his priestly role and presence in local worshipping communities:

> Which are the most reliable companions? Scripture, Eucharist: consistent living in and participation in the church's life is terribly important to me, and constant exposure to that. That's why I really do rely very heavily on the church. For me a lot of these things are like living in a house of abundance and simply drawing on that, rather than going for particular ways of thinking. The abundance is around all the time.

He often felt quite on the margins of things but nevertheless treasured his many years as an Assistant Priest at St Mark's, Londonderry (West Midlands), together with All Saints' (Princeton), Christ Church Canaan (Connecticut) and Great St Mary's (Cambridge); and he found his role as the Van Mildert Canon Professor (Durham University and Cathedral) particularly fulfilling, enabling the academic theologian and the priest in him to come together in new ways. He was also a well-known face at evensong in both St John's and King's College Chapels (Cambridge), which he loved to attend with Perrin whenever he could – right up to the week before he died.

מה-תשתוחחי נפשי ותהמי עלי הוחילי לאלהים
כי עוד אודנו ישועות פניו:

Why are you downcast O my soul?
And why do you throw me into confusion?
Hope in God, for I will yet praise him
for his saving presence. (v. 5)

Worship and praise were fundamentally for God's sake and central to his whole vision and understanding of full human being and society, 'shaping and aligning our desire with the Lord's'.

אלהי עלי נפשי תשתוחח על-כן אזכרך מארץ
ירדן וחרמונים מהר מצער:

תהום-אל-תהום קורא לקול צנוריך כל-משבריך
וגליך עלי עברו:

My God, my soul is downcast.
Therefore I remember you
from the land of Jordan and Hermon and of Mount Mizar.
Deep calls to deep at the sound of your cataracts;
all your breakers and your billows
have gone over me. (vv. 6–7)

At some level he felt (and always had felt) deeply 'unloved': no doubt this was one of the reasons he identified so closely with the marginalized and with the life and work of Samuel T. Coleridge. He had great integrity; he had no time for the games people play (which also had its flip side; he was surprisingly naive and ideal-istic, reluctant almost, when it came to being political); and he always had just as much (if not more) time for the outsider or underdog as he did for the many high-status people he engaged with. This was perhaps something personal to him, but it also had an element of prophetic dissatisfaction about it (see below, p. 22).

Throughout my childhood, I was often aware of a sense of loneliness and heaviness (sadness?) about him and wondered why he had virtually no close personal relationships or friends. He related intellectually with his colleagues and with those for whom he had pastoral care/responsibility, but it was much more difficult for him to share his own feelings and emotions. In later years he sometimes spoke himself of the difficulties he felt he had in communicating, particularly about himself, and in relating to and trusting others. In many ways he was a deeply private and solitary person, with areas that were quite encapsulated[18] and defended within him: he was always responsive, but hardly ever took the initiative, however much you might long for him to (see below, pp. 20, 138 for more on this).

יומם יצוה יהוה חסדו ובלילה שירה עמי תפלה
לאל חיי

By day may the Lord send forth his loving kindness,
so that by night I am with song:
a prayer for the God of my life. (v. 8)

But the work of God's Spirit in him, 'abyss calling to abyss', meant that the black hole (whatever shape or form it took) never had the last word, and, despite times of real darkness, he was not someone who lived in despair; he was always more attracted to the light and able to keep hoping and trusting in God's goodness.

He never regretted his decision to remain in the UK:

People in Oxford encouraged me to look for a teaching position in England, a possibility we had never dreamed of. And there came a time when I was offered two posts: one in England and one in the USA. It became clear that the post in England was the better one. Most positions in US universities offered no opportunity to develop as a theologian, but the one at the

University of Birmingham (England) was the first ever lecture-ship in England in contemporary theology. Finding myself in a good, imaginative department of theology in a major civic university in a Midlands city (the second largest after London) was a wonderful gift. And gradually, never intending to stay long, Perrin and I found ourselves and our family (by now our two daughters (Deb and Jen) and son (Dan) were joined by Chris) increasingly settled and happy. The time and opportunities stretched on, academic work enlarged and became still more fascinating, and life there – the city wrongly described in US guidebooks as 'a smoggy place not worth visiting' – was rich and fulfilling for all of us. It would take some explaining to say why, but the combination of university work and life (including church life) in a place with such cultural and religious variety was wonderful. University, church and city – which in England go well together – mixed in all kinds of ways.

One of the joys over the years was to see a gradual blossoming of friendships and conversation partners towards the end of his life and to see how he was finally able to begin taking the initiative in relationships, which became increasingly intimate and mutual. Particularly significant among these were postgraduate students, the Society for the Study of Theology, the American Academy of Religion, David Ford (starting during Birmingham days) and the Peter–Dan–David threesome that began through CTI and was to become the foundation for Scriptural Reasoning and a new realm of relationships and friendships with those of other faiths and disciplines.

אומרה לאל סלעי למה שכחתני למה קדר אלך
בלחץ אויב:
ברצח בעצמותי חרפוני צוררי באמרם אלי
כל היום איה אלהיך:
מה תשתוחחי נפשי ומה תהמי עלי

I say to God, my rock,
'Why have you forgotten me?
Why must I walk about in gloom,

oppressed by the enemy?'
Killing me to the core,
my oppressors shame me,
taunting me all day long:
'Where is your God?'
Why are you downcast, O my soul?
And why do you throw me into confusion? (vv. 9–12)

But the deeper he went into God, the more aware he was of the light and the beauty and attractiveness of God, the more aware he was of the darkness, too: 'To confess to the light is to acknowledge you've strayed: the light reveals both the grace and the disgrace of creation.'[19]

הוחילי לאלהים
כי-עוד אודנו ישועת פני ואלהי

Hope in God, for I will yet praise him
for his saving presence. (v. 12)

That was always the last word for him: trusting in 'the light [that] shines in the darkness, and the darkness did not overcome it' (John 1.5), in the God who continually turns his face and attention towards us and invites us into our fullest meaning and dignity in and through relationship with him. 'For it is the God who said, "Let light shine out of darkness", who has shone in our hearts to give the light of the knowledge of the glory of God in the face of Jesus Christ' (2 Cor. 4.6).

My father loved the beauty in things. He had a life-long love and hunger for music, opera, theatre, poetry, art and architecture; wherever he was, he would find those things. I have warm and vivid memories of him sitting with his head back and eyes shut, savouring the beauty and wonder of music in a range of settings: the Birmingham Bach Society and CBSO (Birmingham), the Endellion Quartet and others performing in West Road Concert Hall (together with various college chapels in Cambridge), stretched out on the grass at Tanglewood (the summer home of the Boston Symphony Orchestra in Massachusetts). And I remember just as clearly how, whenever the music stopped or an interval started, he would immediately pull out his little notebook to capture the latest thought or insight it had given. He found deep meaning and resonance in nature and the arts; they gave a form and expression that he often struggled to find for himself.

Humour was like that, too: as if it somehow needed to be given permission and a way to find expression in him, and when it was and he laughed, he *laughed* – and his laughter grew as he discovered and let go into the joy and wonder and communication of God. Explosions of laughter and delight would often simply erupt from the study or from the shore of the lake – or wherever it was that he was deep in theological conversation with those closest to him. Playfulness for him was primarily in the realm of 'musement': the acrobatics of abstraction.

The psalm captures well the sense of restlessness about him, perhaps a prophetic dimension of his calling, something ahead of his time, restless for the 'more' of God, living the tensions of the 'already and not yet' of the fulfilment of God's Kingdom: Bonhoeffer's 'penultimate'.[20] He was someone who wrestled with things: there was a deep remedial or reparative dimension to his thinking and yet somehow he never seemed to resolve the problem. He is (already) renowned for his: 'I'm afraid things are just not that simple.' He said, 'I am always reaching for more than what seems to be there or possible, so I am always coming up against the limitations.'

And yet the paradox (as he well recognized) was that the difficult things and times in his life were also blessings and shaped and led him into what often became his greatest strengths and opportunities.

He described how his very critical approach to everything had arisen from both hopes and disappointments much earlier in his life and how these were still at the heart of what motivated his thinking:

> The world should be translucent to the divine: that's what I hope for, but the world does not show itself as it was divinely originated. So I am disappointed when it doesn't: perhaps a little how Moses feels when he comes off the mountain, and

he sees the reality of where humanity is and how and why the world has not continued in God's presence. In a sense it does show the divine, but I am disappointed in the world when it gets overly caught up in its extensity – its sheer spread out-ness – and becomes confused and chaotic. It loses its intensity and the potential for order and containment within that.

We have this polyform world in which we live – and we barely know how to hold it together – this plurality of things and activities of people always in a state of disorder and un-formation. There are two things operating: extensity is the sheer polyformality of things and second is the chaos that comes from that. The first is not emotionally charged: it is just the way things are – but chaos *is*. Since I could do nothing about creation – and I suspend judgement in relation to the 'why' in relation to the natural order – I have had a deep desire to do something about *that* dimension of the chaos, to sort out the disorder: the extensity that lies within the human scope. That's why I did ecclesiology; my whole life and work has been an ecclesiological response to the malaise of extensity. The intensity I seek has a maternal dimension. I seek maternal being in ideas: a light attracting me with its warmth. God has maternal intensity, which extensity does not provide.

His theology could only be reparative because it assumed the light and the will to believe in 'the light that shines in the darkness and has not overcome it' (John 1). 'That's the paradox,' he said, 'the sheer enormity of a light which never overwhelms or coerces us, so that it attracts everyone into its warmth.'

The Episcopal Church (into which he was baptized)[21] has in its baptism service the prayer: 'Give him (or her) an inquiring and discerning heart, the courage to will and to persevere, a spirit to know and to love you, and the gift of joy and wonder in all your works.'

This spirit shone in him increasingly, and especially when he embarked on a pilgrimage to the Holy Land.

Jerusalem 2007

On Easter Day 2007 he set out with members of Great St Mary's Church, where he served as an assistant priest during his time in Cambridge, on a pilgrimage to Jerusalem, which was to change his life. It is difficult to capture here in a way that begins to do justice to what it meant to him: something so 'big' happened that afterwards he was only able to give 'glimpses' of it, often quite fragmented ones. But there was a coming together and new integration of his thinking and feeling, and his imagination and senses were liberated in new ways.

I shall try to follow and quote my father's own narrative (as told to me) as closely as possible.

'The Beginnings': The Jordan

I'd been to Israel a number of times and for different reasons, but mostly for academic study outside of religion. In the 1960s (while I was at Oxford), I went to the Hebrew University for an academic conference on the Philosophy and History of Science – and more recently for an inter-faith conference at the Hartman Institute, but that was also a non-religious visit, even if for inter-faith conversation: both visits had been for reasons other than a full engagement with the Holy Land. So it made a lot of difference to Perrin and me that this was *pilgrimage* to the Holy Land, and I give real credit to those who put the trip together. It was conceived by Yazid Said (who had been born in Nazareth and reared as a Christian, so he knew the situation and place well) in collaboration with others at Great St Mary's, and they planned it well. They were trying to introduce us to the whole situation there, political and historical and religious, and we were confirmed in our desire to do the trip by the way it was organized. We rested quite easily in it . . .

The pilgrimage began at Nazareth where we were taken to the Church of the Annunciation. It seems the intention was to expose us to a place where there had been a divine address – the Annunciation of the angel to Mary – and then there was a sequence of places and events after that: the Sea of Galilee, a boat trip and a visit to some of the shrines along the shores, but these were external, cultural events in a sense – not spiritual.

So it all really began when we went from the guesthouse in Nazareth where we were staying to visit the headwaters of the Jordan . . . a place where people had been *touched*. On the bus on the way I was asked to give a homily on 'The Shaping of Desire' (based on Psalm 42)[22] – and this seemed to strike people quite powerfully. When we got there, there were waters simply 'bubbling up' out of the ground. We all gathered around the place where this 'bubbling up' was happening, and I was asked to read the psalm, 'Like as the heart desireth water brooks . . .' Then we shared a Eucharist with a renewal of baptism vows. There was a strange ambience. It was almost like being encircled by the waters, and, although it wasn't a very polished exercise, there was a basic kind of renewal going on. People were folded into the atmosphere of the place – disappearing and then reappearing in the mists by the waters . . . It showed how we can be incorporated in something beyond ourselves. People realized that something was really happening; it was not just an 'exercise' to be observed, but a drama to enter into. This is when the pilgrimage really began.

At the Headwaters of the Jordan (see colour picture 1)

I've no idea if it was as significant for the others as it was for me, but for me it was the beginning of an experience of the play of light. It was an opening into a new understanding of the dimensions of what is going on: the light really going deep into people and transforming them from within: irradiating them. And I noticed qualitatively different relationships *between* people: people were more open and prepared to engage with one another; it was no longer now a notably social tourist group. And of course it was not only what was happening to and within them, but the way I *saw*.

The Road to Jericho

Security wall on the road to Jericho (see colour picture 2)

After the Jordan, we went down towards Jericho. I'd prepared for it a lot, as I was taking the Eucharist there. It is in the West Bank: a Palestinian area of the Holy Land – land that has already been measured and configured for its use within the divine purpose – that is now surrounded and cordoned off by Israel.

So the notion of Divine Measurement was on my mind and an

important preparation for Jerusalem. What is it to be measured for God's purposes? And what might it mean in this place: Jericho, this precursor to the measured city of Jerusalem? I thought about the notion that the world is ordered in a certain way and the 'Chicago School' understanding of this in phenomenological terms . . . But I also wondered how to move beyond this to something more onto-logical: not just decided by human beings, but an understanding that acknowledges something already given and dwelling in the place. Perhaps there could be another kind of measurement that rests not only on bodies and objective knowledge, but more in line with quantum theory, which is trying to measure things by their position and is relational. This opens up the possibility that divine measurement is not simply about God setting something down in a body and leaving it there, but that there is a more fluid, dynamic view that follows the divine purpose.

And what might this mean for the city of Jerusalem? Perhaps that being measured out as special in God's purposes would not be because it is embodied there in any final sort of way, but because it is a place where something could be learnt and recognized: a dynamic *to be entered into* . . . This would be a hugely significant shift in emphasis and understanding.

But it has also become a very problematic place, a place of deep struggle about something people won't bring to the surface: 'the deep and dark places' (religious, political, social). How do we even begin to think of these things? If the creation of light brings darkness, perhaps holiness creates envy – or greed – a claim to a right of possession and a need to possess God, to be God. Perhaps that is what's at the heart of idolatry and at the heart of the com-petition and fighting that have become such a part of Jerusalem's history.

And what can counter this? A shift from Paul Ricœur's 'human economy' of equivalence and exchange to the 'divine economy' of abundance and excess.[23] God is not competitive: what is best for him is best for us, too. That's the mystery of service: entering and going deeper into relation with God is not about loss and restric-tion, but gain. But there is a great sense of *urgency* about it all.

Entering Jerusalem

Jerusalem overlook: The old city (see colour picture 3)

I found our entry into Jerusalem very powerful: the Holy Mount/ Temple; the Wailing Wall and, even more so (to me), the entrance to the tunnel under the Western Wall. It's not easy to say quite why, but what struck me as we walked down under the excavations of the old wall was the *power* of the place: the most ancient stones of the Temple, leading up to much later ones. It's not the physical mass of the place in itself, but that it is *alive: radiant* with light. There was a Bat Mitzvah taking place down there and a steady stream of people stopping to pray. It gave me the sense of this being the *repository* of God's light. One could see it phenomenologically, but it's far more than that: it takes eyes to see it, that's all. I just found I was embraced *by* the light.

It was the sum total of all this that gave me a sense of the huge power of God's light and energy and how the divine is at work. But the question is, 'How to get it across?!' It's an infinitely probing thing: not so much light's searching as light's penetrating. What is it that attracts someone to something better? The strong

Light on the temple walls (see colour picture 4)

sense I have is that the Goodness simply draws them to something *fuller*. It's an opening and enabling process: an attraction and recognition of the life and source of life within. It is like a granulation of patterns, words, light, senses: things percolating up just like the waters of the Jordan; and a whole range of things coming to the surface, with a new awareness of the simple wonder and beauty of creation and life itself; and with that, the awareness of how little we've 'got it'. So with the light comes sadness and loss but also a yearning to live from this source and to be oriented to it: to the life and health bubbling up deep within. The sense of sorrow is sharing in the grief of God and his longing for the best for his people and the world: longing for us not to be distracted or to waste time. It's about recognizing how much more there is than you've ever seen before and being attracted by it and lifted up to it. This light is something that's capable of lifting you deeply from within: the word I've used a lot for it is simply 'attraction'.

Something about the light is its openness and not being exclusive; its being open is inherent to it. We can't contain the light however much we might want to or try to. Remember YHWH: 'I am who I

The 'Dominus Flevit' Chapel (the site where 'the Lord wept over Jerusalem')
(see colour picture 5)

am and I shall be who I shall be . . .' Our human attempts to hold
and define God become inimical to the light. We cannot grasp hold:
like trying to grasp Israel for the Jews. It is one thing to have a
homeland, but it's quite another to possess it and restrict it. Think
what it's like to have a child: it's a *gifting of responsibility.*

So what is it to indwell somewhere and have a homeland without possessing it? How can we participate honestly in the huge
reality of the light without needing to possess it? The divine light
is lifting you to something you don't need to possess: it is lifting
you to another sphere. It enters you non-possessively and filters up
within you. We're regenerated – transformed and rebuilt – from
deep within.

People don't believe things can be renewed in that way. They're
too stuck, too fixed; that's the heavy imprint of materialism that
most people live with. But what if we were freed from that? What
if we were given new categories and could shift away from the
Aristotelian fixed units of measure to something new altogether?
Into a sphere of indefinite possibility and the realization that this
energy can reshape and redefine everything from within? That's

the language of the resurrection: measurement is redefined. It is not pre-ordained things, plans or units that define, but *this* 'unit' of the most primal energies – the life and energy of the Spirit. I wrote a paper once, while I was at the Center of Theological Inquiry. It was never published, but it was uniquely important for me: 'Spirit of Creation, Reconciled'. It taught me the power and depth of the Spirit that I hadn't grasped before: that the Spirit is primary in the Trinity, the bedrock of the Trinity. It was quite a shift for me. I think, like most people, I had a fairly conventional notion of it until then, seeing the Spirit as a sort of add-on dimension to the Trinity, not deeply intrinsic to it. But then I began to realize that it is much more fundamental. I began to recognize it as the energy of the divine: always there at the beginning and before the beginning, right at the heart of God.

People are often habitually drawn away from the light. So how, with all the leaves falling, covering it up and burying the light, how do we uncover it? This is our tragedy: extensity. We're caught up in this thing after that thing and then another thing. When we meet someone who is open and drawn into this light – whose eyes are opened to see – it's not just their personal experience. Something is happening in that person on behalf of humanity and he/she is making an authentic contribution: fulfilling something vital. People lose and miss the significance of who they are and what their purpose is. Sharing is important because if something good is not shared, something is missed. It's about us sharing and participating in the depths of God and God's goodness, indefinitely and infinitely. That's where things get really exciting: there's a depth in God that is fathomless. That's where it gets quite dazzling: what might be! The infinite potential of the world. We limit ourselves so much! But the invitation is to get caught up in the re-creative Spirit of the divine: the Trinity.

The world has huge potential that it's sunk away from. But it's important not to focus on the remedial: to focus, instead, on the huge *potential*: God's goodness and Spirit at work in and among us! We need to be clever in the ways of the world and to see what's gone wrong – and even perhaps why – but not get stuck there. It's a matter of identifying the blocks and then moving on. It's easy to get stuck in the blockages rather than focusing on the

Marc Chagall's 'The Tribe Simeon' window at the Hadassah Hospital Synagogue, Jerusalem[24] (see colour picture 6)

wonder and glory and vision of God and getting swept up and caught up in it. It's not a matter of us working out 'how'.

There is a strong temporal thrust of movement forward, a perfecting movement towards the fullness of God's creation and God's work, far beyond what we can see. What is the fullness of God's work with the world?[25] That's plainly what it's all directed to: there's a huge panoply of things that need to be attended to.[26] The dynamic is there, but we have to participate in it and identify what's involved in it. It's partly a matter of being swept up in and by it, but it's also a matter of acknowledging that these responsibilities are there. So often we get distracted. What is it that both attracts and limits the Church? It has become over-concentrated on its inner meaning. We need to learn how to persist with our task in the world. What are the essentials of this? Opening up the true potential and resources of human life: liturgy is one way of facilitating and helping people to enter into this creative dynamic and drawing them deeper into the light, letting it penetrate them and 'irradiate' them. But it's certainly not exclusive to the Church; there are lots of other ways, too, and we need to recognize and interpret them in public life. It's about how the Church relates to the world.

Emerging from the Walls: From Jerusalem to Sinai and Home

After emerging from the tunnel we went beyond the Wailing Wall and then back to where we were staying. Until this point we had been one whole group, but this was the end of the trip for most people, so we had a time of re-gathering and recollection before saying farewell to those who were about to leave. It was a significant time of sharing, listening to what different people had made of it all, and those of us who'd decided to go on went back to Bethlehem, where we had had a day visit earlier in the trip.

Emerging from the tunnel under the Wailing Wall (see colour picture 7)

It was appalling to see how reduced the Palestinians had become: from our chintzy purpose-built hotel we could see all too clearly the huge wall that has been built to serve as a barrier to any communication between Bethlehem and Israel. It was deeply symbolic – and it was ominous, with sections of concrete abutted together.

So it was a strange thing. We were sort of suspended into this unbelievably posh hotel, and we spent the night there, surrounded by elegant showrooms where we had the opportunity to buy whatever we might have wanted. But we could do absolutely nothing, until leaving on a bus for Sinai early the next morning.

It was a very, very long trip – way down past the Dead Sea – and there were a few minor stops. By then I was finding it all pretty gruelling; perhaps that's when I realized I was getting too tired.

I had toyed with the idea of going up Sinai, but that wouldn't have been the wise thing to do. Ideally I'd have loved to, and some did: setting off in the dark early hours – some opting for camels – and then when they came down we spent a good part of the day around the monastery there, built over the site of the burning bush.

It looks like it was just another step in a tourist trip. But it wasn't. It had become a pilgrimage when right back at the Jordan people realized they were inside the whole thing, being re-baptized. Then it wasn't simply an exterior thing, but their *own* drama. So at the monastery at Sinai, although it could all have been treated as a museum experience, it was something much deeper. It was about a reality confronting you that was far more impressive than conventional philosophy will allow.

The monastery sitting at the base of Sinai isn't just an interesting geological artefact. It's an impressive ancient Christian monastery: hugely significant for Christians and Jews and filled with connections. It has a Jewish presence there, and there is no over-rating its huge importance for Jews: it is not possessed and remains a vivid reminder of Moses' encounter with YHWH at the burning bush. This is the burning, living bush, the living presence of God. The monastery is called 'The Monastery of the Divine Fire'. It is a very special place; in a sense, it's almost a bore-hole into the divine fire, with the light that goes with it: a place of ongoing light.

The Monastery of the Divine Fire at Mt. Sinai (see colour picture 8)

It's a place of transfiguration, hinting at an unending source of light: the 'I am that I am'. What does that mean? That there's an 'I am' always reaching back to a further 'I am', and there's no end to that process. It's often taken as a statement of ontology, but it's more than that if you go into it. It takes you further into the 'I am' and into the infinity of the light that emerges. For years, I've found that to be the most nourishing thing of all: that there's no sudden halt to the direction you can go; there's always more, and that is pretty unquestionably linked to the light. The simple resplendence of the light here paralleled my experiences in Palestine.

It is amazing, the burning bush: it's a primitive 'symbol' and yet it is not consumed. It means that the divine can indwell the world without damaging it or taking it over. The transfiguration is more complex, but what supervenes them all is this enormous light. If you think of creation as in some sense a breaking through of the light, there are real parallels with the transfiguration and with the end times, with the unifying, consistent theme being the light, with its gentle and yet strong attraction.

How do healing and reconciliation happen? This light heals without overburdening; that's not in its nature. Christians often want a strong right arm. They talk in the language of power, but that's not what it's about; it's about a gentle infiltration from within, not coming at you from outside, like a ton of bricks.

How does light happen within the world? It irradiates from within. It's like seeing people 'light up' within; it's a huge privilege, and we have to recognize and discern it in one another and to embrace and delight in it.

That's what working with postgraduates is about: gently edging forward the things that are being prompted in them. Things take on a new kind of tentativeness. It's about letting them recognize and articulate for themselves what is happening and what it is that they're a part of; that's the wonder. That's what Jesus did. He didn't say, 'Here I am: this is what to do . . .' He didn't come with the purpose of giving a standard or doctrine; he *met* with people, and the meeting has to show itself as deeply as possible, to reveal who he is for – and in relationship with – each person. Read the Gospels: suspend your judgement and let him come alive afresh. I've learnt a lot in the last month about how Jesus happens for people. I've moved from understanding Jesus as a given who presents himself to you – and you can either take him or leave him – to realizing that it's much more about Jesus walking alongside people and interacting with them/us. It opens up a much bigger space with Jews and Muslims: walking with Jesus allows you to walk with other traditions. It provides a wonderful opening because you can imagine Jesus walking with others, too. It's a triple hermeneutic as Jesus meets with Jews and Muslims too. Just imagine the Emmaus Road story as a story of Jesus coming and walking among his disciples: Christian, Jew and Muslim. Simply look at all the things that Jesus did: his 'love statements' opening out the light in things and people, just being there in the flesh with them.

Coming Home (Back to my voice!)

This is where my father ended his 'narrative' account of his pilgrimage to Jerusalem.

He returned home full of the Spirit. Something so powerful and deep had happened that afterwards (every day) he could not rest until he had found ways to do justice to it and to articulate more of it. Now there was a sense of Jeremiah's 'within me there is something like a burning fire shut up in my bones; I am weary with holding it in, and I cannot'[27] – but with more of the praise and wonder of the Magnificat ('My soul magnifies the Lord, and my spirit rejoices in God my Saviour'), too!

He had a new conviction of his purpose and deepest vocation and identity, and he was swept up in articulating the profound glimpse of the light and glory of God he had had during the pilgrimage.[28] There was a new sense of integration and ability to articulate, too.

But he also returned with an unexplained and never-before sense of exhaustion: 'I don't know what's the matter with me: I've never felt so tired in my whole life. Maybe it's just because I'm getting older and I'll pick up again when I get some rest . . .' But he didn't. When I asked him to describe what it felt like (on the way to the hospital), he said, 'Usually my mind is reaching out for things – for ideas and information: all the time, but now it's as if I can't . . .' And within days he was diagnosed with an aggressive brain tumour. A friend, who is a doctor, said to us: 'Just pray it's not a GBM.'[29] But it was. All he needed was enough time, and from that moment he began to talk with Peter every day about the contents – 'their part' – of this book.

Notes

1 'Now on that same day two of them were going to a village called Emmaus . . . and talking with each other about all these things that had happened. While they were talking and discussing, Jesus himself came near and went with them, but their eyes were kept from recognizing him' (Luke 24.13ff.).

2 At the time of writing I do not have enough distance on his life and death to be able to call him anything but 'my father'.

3 Cf. Arvo Pärt (one of his favourite composers): 'I could compare my music to white light which contains all colours. Only a prism can divide the colours and make them appear; this prism could be the spirit of the listener' (*On Alina*: Spiegel im Spiegel, ECM New Series 1591, 449 958–2, ECM Records GmbH 1999).

4 Micheal O'Siadhail, *Hail! Madam Jazz*, Newcastle upon Tyne: Bloodaxe Books, 1992, p. 14.

5 K. Barth, *Church Dogmatics* IV.I, Edinburgh: T and T Clark, 1958.

6 'Truly my life is one long hearkening unto myself and unto others and

unto God. And if I say hearken, it is really God who hearkens inside me. The most essential and deepest in me hearkening unto the most essential and deepest in the other. God to God' (Etty Hillesum, *An Interrupted Life and Letters and Papers from Westerbork*, New York: Henry Holt and Company, 1995, p. 204).

'When I pray, I hold a silly, naïve, or deadly serious dialogue with what is deepest inside me, which for sake of convenience I call God . . . I repose in myself. And that part of myself, that deepest and richest part in which I repose, is what I call "God"' (Hillesum, *Interrupted Life*, p. xv).

7 A deep infection of the bone – in his case, his left shin, following a soccer injury.

8 Doctorate of Divinity.

9 *Jubilate: Theology in Praise*, London: Darton, Longman & Todd, 1984. Now available under the title *Living in Praise: Worshipping and Knowing God*, second edition, London: Darton, Longman & Todd, 2005. Also published in the USA as *Praising and Knowing God*, Louisville, KY: Westminster Press, 1985.

10 Published 13 October 2007.

11 Ephesians 3.14ff.

12 'Scriptural reasoning or SR for short, refers to a way in which those of different faiths share their scriptures together, originally derived from a practice called "*textual* reasoning" among a group of Jewish scholars out of which *Scriptural* Reasoning has evolved. It's a way in which Christians, Muslims and Jews share their scriptures together (texts from the Bible, the Qur'an and the Tanakh – often quite difficult and challenging texts). What makes it work is the very open, trusting and enquiring *spirit* within which it is done. One of the ways Dan described it was "discovering the patterns of Scripture and how they relate to patterns within other faiths".' For further information about Scriptural Reasoning visit http://etext.lib.virginia.edu/journals/jsrforum/pastconferences.html (University of Virginia). There is also a film: http://www.pbs.org/wnet/religionandethics/week1106/cover.html. SR is growing fast in a number of countries around the world as a means of inter-faith dialogue.

13 My father died during the week when he had hoped to be at the annual SR gathering at the American Academy of Religion. Days before, when I told him that Peter wanted to come to see him, he protested (knowing how much SR meant to Peter) that he should go San Diego instead. When Peter decided to come anyway, he was only pacified when we agreed that we would do SR here, so that he could be part of it too. Sadly, Peter arrived just after he had died, but it seemed very fitting to honour this commitment anyway.

14 The New Jerusalem Bible suggests that 'the land of Jordan and Hermon' (v. 6) might refer to a place/stage on the route of the Israelites in exile.

15 Daniel Hardy, 'Thoughts on a lifetime so far', unpublished paper.

16 But he was later deeply encouraged by the appointment and vision of Will Storrar as one of his successors there.

17 When we discussed various options for his funeral, he said adamantly: 'The most important thing is that it's an act of worship, and that the person and place facilitate that.'

18 'Autistic' in the psychoanalytic sense of the word: see Frances Tustin, *The Protective Shell in Children and Adults*, London: Karnac, 1990.

19 See Chapter 5, pp. 102–03.

20 Dietrich Bonhoeffer, *Ethics*, New York: Macmillan, 1955, p. 125.

21 St George's Church, Flushing.

22 Only at the time of writing did it dawn on me that this was the psalm we studied together at the vigil before his funeral (see above).

23 Paul Ricœur, *Figuring the Sacred: Religion, Narrative and the Imagination*, Minneapolis: Fortress Press, 1995.

24 'Simeon and Levi are brothers; weapons of violence are their swords. May I never come into their council; may I not be joined to their company–for in their anger they killed men, and at their whim they hamstrung oxen. Cursed be their anger, for it is fierce, and their wrath, for it is cruel! I will divide them in Jacob, and scatter them in Israel' (Gen. 49.5–7). Image © ADAGP, Paris and DACS, London 2010.

25 The notion of praise as 'perfecting perfection' can be found in *Jubilate / Living in Praise*.

26 See the Receptive Ecumenism website, http://www.centreforcatholicstudies. co.uk/?cat=6, as well as the recent volume: Paul D. Murray, ed., *Receptive Ecumenism and the Call to Catholic Learning: Exploring a Way for Contemporary Ecumenism* (Oxford: Oxford University Press, 2008).

27 Jeremiah 20.9.

28 He later described the very nature and purpose of pilgrimage as 'discovering one's purpose and desire' (see Chapter 2).

29 *Glioblastoma multiforme*.

PART TWO

An Ecclesiology of Pilgrimage

Daniel W. Hardy (as told to Peter Ochs)

2

At the Headwaters of the Jordan: The Energetics of Personal Transformation

Narrative

Our defining experience at the headwaters was the Baptismal Eucharist, shaped – at least for me – by our reading and interpretation of Psalm 42: 'As a deer thirsts for flowing streams, so my soul thirsts for you, O God. My soul thirsts for God, for the living God. When shall I come and behold the face of God?'[1] The experience was extraordinary, not simply because we combined baptism and Eucharist (that is commonplace), but because they were united and enacted in a particularly fulsome way at an extraordinary place (the headwaters of the Jordan) and time (the 'head' or beginning of our trip). Experiencing the Eucharist at a place of such importance brought home to the group the magnitude of what they were about to do on this pilgrimage.

In a typical service, psalms and prayers come first, then the sermon, followed by the baptism and finally culminating in the Eucharist. Here, because of the place and the setting, there was a difference. The setting was alongside an up-rush of water that flows out of a cave: the cave is in the background, and in the foreground a rush of water floods a pool of about ten feet across, two feet deep. A site was already prepared here for religious exercises: an altar set up permanently about 15 to 20 feet from the water. People congregated in a circle around the altar, standing. The priest officiated at the altar in the middle of the circle. Adjusting the order of service to the order of our pilgrimage, I offered a preparatory psalm (42) on the bus before we arrived. Then we gathered around the altar for readings and prayers, followed by a renewal of baptism in the waters. People took water from the Jordan by themselves or with the help of others, and everyone reaffirmed their baptismal vows by pouring water over their own heads: everyone except for the priest, whose son-in-law was present and performed this service for her. It was particularly moving to see this: our priest experiencing a renewal of life through the hands of her son-in-law. They did this quietly (they are the understated British after all!), and then returned to our circle around the altar, where we proceeded with a full celebration of the Eucharist.

From Narrative to Theology

The purpose of a pilgrimage is the renewal of identities. In this sense, the baptismal service marked the formal beginning of our pilgrimage. It was a time for all members of the journey to restart their identities and thus renew the pilgrimage itself. That ties in closely to thinking of pilgrimage as a vessel that moves us from being unknown to having an identity. Pilgrimage is an enactment: a particular kind of encounter that has particular consequences, primary among which is the emergence of identity, both on the part of the One with whom the encounter occurs and the one who is having the encounter: God and person. It is a mutual act of identification of God and of the pilgrim that cannot be sufficiently captured in doctrinal assertions but is recognized only in the ongoing encounter and the identities that emerge from it.

Pilgrimage and the education of desire

I learned from this stage of our pilgrimage that this encounter between God and human has something to do with the formation of desire. Having begun to open up Psalm 42 ('As a deer thirsts for flowing streams, so my soul thirsts for you, O God') together on our bus journey, I went on to offer a small homily about the education of desire, and this served as a reference point about what would happen at the headwaters of the Jordan. It served to reinterpret the re-baptism our group was about to enact. I described desire as the transformation of affections, the way the affections are directed. By 'affection' I meant anything that eventuates in passion. Coleridge had planned to show that people follow certain cognitive trajectories in life and that there is also an affective trajectory they follow; these two should eventually coincide in a fully formed human being, a human being that has integrity. All this happens through the attraction of the divine. In being attracted to the divine (in what we call 'abduction', to be explained below), these two parts of the person come together, an integration that cannot be articulated in Lockean or Kantian categories (although Kant's effort is the more helpful).

The affections begin in brute human nature as arbitrary, but they then become focused. Focused on their proper objects, the affections appear no longer as simply cravings, but now as something fundamental and deep: a desire for the wellbeing of the other. How does higher reason relate to affection? Each informs the other. Because of his heroin addiction, Coleridge experienced a conflict between his high conceptual ability and his need for moral transformation. He discovered the two cannot be separated, reason and the passions each inform the other.

Baptism and affection

Our baptism at the headwaters of the Jordan signalled the beginning of our enacting a pilgrimage that until then was only latent in our trip. For me, the enactment began in a specific moment: the activity of pouring water over my own head. Stooping over this rushing water and pouring it over my head marked a point of transition, when our 'trip to the Holy Land' became a spiritual pilgrimage. In retrospect, I became aware of distinct elements of the pilgrimage after I became aware of distinct elements from the baptism: the elements of head, water, hands. I also became aware of specific actions, such as extending the hand forward. But the defining moment of awareness was of a physical sensation: 'It is cold! It is more than just water. It seems to be alive.' The waters poured into an impressed area by the cave, so that when the area was filled, I was surrounded by waters full of life, so I was filled as well by the most vivid sense that, when I reached in to draw a handful, what I touched was not merely H_2O, but also a regathering of the life that is within the waters.

In Coleridgian terms, what I sensed was a concentration of thought occurring there. Before the baptism, the idea of pilgrimage was only cognitive for me, without any attention to the affections. I had anticipated pilgrimage in a 'cool way', my thoughts 'independent' of desire. But through that moment of scooping up the baptismal water, what had been merely thought became an instrument of desire. The enactment of pilgrimage meant an awakening of the affections.

Interlude: What I desire: Society's embrace

Usually, I think of myself in cognitive ways. If I think of myself, it is in terms of thought alone. Rather than having my self-description overwhelmed by emotion, my strategy is to get back to the common-sense level and to sort out the facts: a strategy of thought. When those around me talk 'hot', my reaction is to be the 'coolest', so I can find out what is going on. But one cannot simply rationalize this way. One needs to sense or feel and experience light and desire, as well as to think them.

On this pilgrimage my own desire was for total reorientation: a desire to see more deeply. This is partly a desire to be with and appreciate the other: passionate thought that is somehow fully in the presence of the other. I wish for the proximity of embrace – with what is human, but also with all things, all being embraced illustratively. It is almost a tactile sense: this embrace could include physical touch, but not only literally. Touching the ground, touching the water, touching the soul are examples of this touch. The desire to be enclosed by another, human and non-human. This desire is associated very much with society: the desire to be enclosed within and embraced by society. Society offers a more comprehensive way of embracing than individuals do, and this applies to one's embrace of all being and the world as well. Society works this very way: by bringing its members more affectively into touch with each other. The very purpose of society is to show how embrace happens.

The baptismal waters

The desire for water awakens in people their deeper desires and their deeper sense of divine integrity. Pilgrimage is an awakening to desire for one's own integrity. To see water – and, in this moment, the waters – is to see one of two things: either you see something individual and discrete, visible in its discreteness, or you see something that serves as a possible occasion for relationship with others. To see the waters is to see an occasion either for separation and individuality or for integration, unity and coming together. What made that day at the Jordan so integrative and significant for me was that the bubbling waters I touched became reminders of the bubbling within, a bubbling of inner disruption and of inner intensity. Touching the waters opened poetic analogies between the waters outside and in. I believe our prior study of Psalm 42 ('As a deer thirsts for flowing streams, so my soul thirsts for you, O God') somehow prepared me for this experience of the waters: I preached on how the education of desire translates some narrative outside us into something that is inside. But my own sense of that lesson remained cognitive until the waters. Touching the waters brought that lesson inside, drawing together the outer discreteness and inner intensity. So it is possible to redescribe the ritual order of our pilgrimage as having provided a setting for this transformation.

Pilgrimage as being churched

We might name and outline the whole sequence as follows: *Pilgrimage transformed from an external act to an internal one: beginning the deep pilgrimage.* The pilgrimage is initiated by a ritual of the Word, including baptism and Eucharist. The next step is 'being churched'. When a woman gives birth, and four days after has purification and re-entry, we say 'she is churched', that is, 'she is purified from that in which she is impure'. In these terms, one could say that our group was 'churched' at the headwaters of the Jordan. For each person, baptism in the headwaters integrated inner extensity and intensity, by analogy with the extensity of the waters and the intensity of our inner transformation.

Ecclesiology: The Energetics of Personal Transformation

Attraction: Drawn by the light

So, my inner pilgrimage really began when, at the headwaters of the Jordan, my affections were aroused and my thought about God was transformed into desire for God. Pilgrimage is the arousal and education of desire for God. Displaced from its self-directedness, the self is attracted elsewhere, from its own relative darkness to the light that it comes to know through the name of God. When redescribed in the context of a general ecclesiology, this arousal of movement toward God may be named 'attraction'.

I would define attraction, first, as 'being drawn to and by'. For Coleridge, attraction refers to the word in the spirit, which means that the 'being drawn' is given its impetus by an ordered energy.[2] The word in the spirit is the means by which things are drawn into union. This is the absolute core of the energetics of attraction – and the core of what I have diagrammed in Figure 1: there is an ordered energy that is perpetually self-generative and fully self-replenishing all the time. We use labels like 'ordered energy', or 'word in spirit', or 'Trinity', or 'God', but these are not just labels for something that is there. They name that which of its nature is infinite, endless and expansive, to which the only possible response is not to name it but to follow it into the depths. You can say of it only that it is what attracts.

This is the overwhelming sensation I have: this perpetual process of going more and more deeply into that which attracts without ever exhausting it. As one goes on, one finds an endless energy associated with it, which I name 'light'. I feel as if I could reach with my arms and just gather in the light, as though it were something that could be swept into one's grasp but which in fact could not be grasped. Or as if I could sweep it to someone so that it enfolded and enriched that person. It is like the sensation of praying for somebody: associating the light with them by sweeping one's arm around the light and pushing it in their direction. That is my prayer.

This is how one responds to the depths that lie at the core of attraction.

There is another way to characterize attraction: as the direction of creatures toward their creator, so we see that creatures are not created 'moving away' from the creator but moving toward him. God creates things toward him, not away from him.

I resist the idea that God just causes things, as if they were fabricated as separate entities. Things are not caused in the sense of being fabricated. They are created toward God, and they must be allowed to participate fully in that to which they are toward. If one thinks of the source of things as light, then you might say that things are themselves in the light, so that their very stuff shows the radiance of light. I suppose this is what underlies my awareness of the shining stones in Jerusalem (the subject of Chapter 5). Things are themselves, but not as fabricated things; things are created, rather, to be radiant, to be full of the divine. I am not suggesting emanationism. Things are as radiant as the light; in that sense, they are full of the divine. We are to understand their appearance as no more than the coming of the light.[3] We do not know what it means for something to be created: the most we can say is that to be created is to be dispersed; creation is the dispersion of things, and it is this dispersion that is attractive.[4] Another term for the dispersion is 'matter'.[5] Attraction thus refers to the way that creatures are drawn toward the creator, drawn thereby to other creatures by way of their bodily existence.

Within a theology of redemption 'attraction' names the movement through which things that are in need of redemption re-establish what I call their 'towardness', which is the direction of creation. Creatures are created to move toward God. When creatures somehow lose that towardness – becoming obsessive at some point, separating from the whole of things and serving only themselves – then the creation loses its order. To lack attraction to others and to God is to suffer the inertia of self-attraction: in Luther's terms, to be 'twisted into self'. Things need redemption when, twisted into themselves, they have lost their towardness. Attraction is redemptive because it restores the directionality of things and, thereby, restores the integrity of creation. If, for example, any denominations serve themselves rather than the whole Church, or if any interpreters claim, 'We have the whole meaning of the Bible, not just one perspective,' then they move against God's attraction.

Any time one is aware of even an inkling of the badness of things, one has already started on the way to redemption. One has acknowledged that something is awry in creation and thus has an inkling of how to re-establish the towardness of things. Towardness is even more basic than creation and redemption. The very nature of things *is* towardness. One cannot expunge towardness from the condition of things.

Inspired by Coleridge's efforts to diagram elemental relations, Figure 1 offers a diagram of the energetics of attraction in our broadest ecclesiology: a diagram of the arrows of attraction that draw each element of civilization to God and that animate the various dimensions of God's relation to us.[6] Notice that each arrow points from the creator toward the creature and from one dimension of creaturely and civilizational life to another. Attraction points from the head of any arrow (the direction of creation as dispersion) toward its shaft (the direction of attraction back

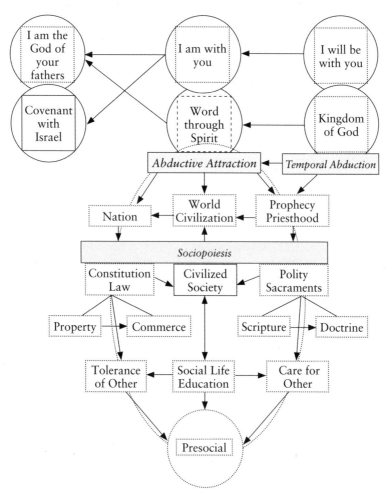

Figure 1: The Energetics of Attraction

to the creator). Everything is toward God, attracted to God. All creatures are attracted to God. Angels are unremittingly attracted; they are God's means of drawing creatures into attraction. They are holy beings, more filled with the fullness of attraction than we can imagine.

The activity of being attracted is something within the creature, not outside it; it belongs to the creature's very being as created.

Creatures have a seed of perfection in them antecedently: a capacity for benevolence, for being attracted and thus for being brought into relation with their creator. Not to be attracted is, against the direction of creation, to be enclosed in one's self-reference. To be attracted is to be drawn beyond oneself to God. It is also to be drawn to others throughout the order of creation. This attraction to others characterizes the inherent sociality of all creation: the irresistible attraction of each creature to others. 'Sociopoiesis' – the generation and shaping of relations – is not something that has to be fabricated. Sociopoiesis operates in the divine, so that it is a dimension of all things always. That is why theories of social construction are inadequate. They lay waste to the divine by veiling the divine presence in all sociality and by burdening humanity with a task beyond its capacity: to bring creatures into relation independently of the powers of attraction.

Sociopoiesis could not be there if it were not there from the beginning in God. The beginning is always there. Creation means the beginning is ever present. Sociopoiesis is always in the divine energy as opposed to being fabricated, constructed, evolved, conditioned, or caused by something. This means that sociopoiesis is 'abductive', as I shall now explain.

Abduction

Coleridge introduced the term 'abduction' to refer to the capacity of our reasoning to be drawn by light, enabling us to 'see' more than perception allows. Abduction draws on the inner light of reason, *lumina rationale*, generating what Hooker called 'divinely infused rationality'. Drawing (most probably) on Coleridge's term, the philosopher Charles Peirce identified 'abduction' as the mode of reasoning – which is distinct from deduction and induction – that generates probabilistic claims about the world: from everyday guesses about which dress to wear, or what door to open, to scientific hypotheses: to our deepest 'wagers' about the reality of God – wagers like Pascal's, on which we are prepared to stake our lives.[7] But Coleridge never conceives of abduction operating apart from relation to God. For him, whatever the subject and level of reasoning – cognitive, relational, appetitive, moral, somatic – reasoning beyond the proximate always means reasoning in relation to the divine light. At the same time, the divine is always implicated in whatever it transforms. For Coleridge, every knowing and all love involve abduction, from chaotic spontaneity, to the most rudimentary kind of volition, to the highest form, which is love. All knowing and all love involve abduction, drawing the whole person closer to the divine light and thus closer to all things; and the whole person includes all modes of personal activity: cognition, politics, relations, ethics, economics and love.

In my ecclesiology, I adopt Coleridge's sense of the term 'abduction' to identify our capacity to turn away from self-engagement back to our primordial attraction to others and to God. Collectively, this is the capacity of any group of creatures to resume sociopoiesis, extending the fields of attraction that generate and coordinate ever-expanding circles and patterns of relation, ordering the group but also reaching past it to other groups and individuals and ultimately to all creatures and all created worlds. While abduction operates on all these levels, we engage in abduction more self-consciously when we are aware of something incompletely explained or not explained at all; abduction opens our capacity to answer questions that cannot otherwise be answered. If we are indeed self-aware, then we will recognize that this is always a capacity to reason, and to reason through attraction to others and to God. While creation is dispersion, abduction is an activity of concentration. As illustrated in Figure 1, it is reasoning's passage from the 'head' toward the origin of each arrow. Unless inhibited by self-attraction, this passage is stimulated by any question or engagement with the unexplained. More dramatic episodes of reasoning are stimulated by more dramatic engagements with the unknown. There are times, for example, when a group's very language cannot account for what has happened in the world. At such times, abduction may lead to transformations not only in the vocabulary but also in the very grammar and syntax of a group's language. Abduction is the means through which sociopoiesis regenerates whatever levels of relation are challenged by uncertainty or the unknown. To the degree that we are self-engaged, the unknown appears to us as that which lies outside the limits of our knowledge and thus ourselves. Interrupting such self-engagement, abduction leads us beyond our self-understanding and our customary practices. It leads beyond the proximate, transforming what appears fixed and bounded into something much more fluid. To the degree that we allow self-displacement, abduction opens us indefinitely into ever-new relations to the other. Re-engaging us in our primordial attraction to God, abduction opens us again to taking on characteristics of the divine. We may begin not only to engage in relations with the other, but also to awaken our sympathy for the other and ultimately work for the improvement of the other.[8] Working on all levels of our being – cognitive, relational, appetitive, moral, somatic – abduction both retains and transforms each characteristic of our personhood. Abduction does not therefore quiet the appetites; it transforms them into desire for God and thus desire for the other's wellbeing.

Figure 1 diagrams the elemental movements of abduction in civilizational sociopoiesis, as displayed in the different ways people *are raised* to flourishing as a society. (If they are self-referential, they will say they 'raise themselves'.) The diagram should be read along three trajectories. On the left side, there are (a) a nation formed through its constitution and political process, (b) incorporating citizens who are educated so as (c) to tolerate each other and care for their basic needs. In the middle, there are (a) a global society that arises from the formation of civilized society, (b) incorporating people who are socialized to accept responsibility for each other, thereby (c) drawing people out of their presocial, self-preoccupied ways into relations of care and provision for each other. On the right side, there are (a) a Church formed through its constitution and polity, including the mutual engagement of the faithful with those ordained to guide them. The Church thereby (b) socializes its people, (c) with the purpose of learning the truth of others, through the deepest care for them. Through these means, the Church moves civilization by way of prophecy and priesthood toward the Kingdom of God. These trajectories are mutually implicated in ways that are overlooked by those who would define modern society and the Church as independent or even mutually exclusive. Many of these mutual implications are shown by arrows in the chart. The head of each arrow shows the direction of energy: ← indicates that the attractive energy comes from a source shown to the right; → indicates the reverse; while ↔ indicates mutual influence.

Where it occurs, sociopoiesis is built on certain preconditions, which are indicated by downward arrows in the diagram (↓). Social life, for example, presupposes presocial life. At the same time, sociopoiesis as a whole is also generated by influences intrinsic to its own movement. These inner influences are indicated by upward arrows (↑). Social life, for example, draws on the attractive energies of civilized society, and 'care for the other' draws on the energies of the ecclesial polity and sacraments.

The arrows also indicate more specific features of each relation. The head of each arrow (← or ↓) points to the inner 'content' of a particular mode of sociality, while the shaft indicates that this content is to be read with reference to a given source or influence. For example, 'tolerance of others' names the social consequences of certain 'laws' within a given constitutional system; while church 'doctrine' indicates how 'Scripture' speaks to certain questions of belief and action. Conversely, the direction from the arrow shaft toward its head indicates that a certain source of attractive energy (such as 'Scripture') needs to be mediated by the material contents of certain consequents (such as 'doctrine'). Looking broadly, for example, at the right and left trajectories of the diagram, 'global civilization' (on the left) has meaning with reference to 'prophecy and priesthood', while the latter derive their material content from 'global civilization': prophecy speaks *into* – or within – a civilization to call it to something better; priesthood stands with a civilization to relate it to that by which it is perfected. 'Prophecy and priesthood' thus *transform* global civilization; through this process, they acquire and display their worldly character and force.

For the purposes of this book, significant lessons are to be learnt by considering the vertical relations between the circle of society and the divine life. The diagram indicates that there is much more to sociopoiesis than the interaction of human institutions, since the energetics of attraction that animate sociopoiesis have their source in the divine life. As indicated in the upper-right side of the diagram, the Kingdom of God is embodied in our temporal plane through the word and actions of prophecy and priesthood. Conversely, prophecy and priesthood open a polity to the Kingdom of God by way of what I call 'temporal abduction': divinely infused reasoning that discloses to a given generation how in their time and place they will best serve the Kingdom of God and contribute to its realization. This abduction lends sociopoiesis its directionality in temporal history. As indicated in the upper-left side of the diagram, the Kingdom opens attractive energy to the spirit-filled Word of God, animating the Word's embodiment in national and global civilization. Conversely, national and global civilization open a law-governed society to the spirit-filled Word by way of what I call 'abductive attraction': divinely infused reasoning that discloses to a given society how its juridical and political institutions will best embody the divine Word. This abduction lends sociopoiesis its instructional and legal wisdom.

The abductive dimension of pilgrimage

As we have seen, my ecclesiology addresses itself not only to 'the Church' in a self-limited sense, but also to sociopoiesis throughout all of God's creation, where sociopoiesis refers to the capacity for generating ever-expanding orders of relation. In *God's Ways with the World*, I considered sociopoiesis in its broadest sense. In *Finding the Church*, I considered sociopoiesis within the context of ecclesial history and, in particular, of Anglican history and polity. In this volume, I ground sociopoiesis in a eucharistic pneumatology of the Church and then I examine the potential uses of such a sociopoiesis as a prototype of human society, Western society in particular. One central claim of this chapter is that sociopoiesis is immanent in each creature and is inhibited only through a creature's inertia or self-absorption. Another central claim is that sociopoiesis is immanent as each creature's primordial attraction to its creator. When that attraction is veiled by a creature's self-attraction, then the creature is in need of redemption. To be redeemed is to recover one's attraction to God, which includes attraction to the other and to all others. I employ Coleridge's term 'abduction' to refer to the divinely infused rationality that re-opens the self-absorbed human being to attraction.

In these terms, we may redefine 'pilgrimage' as an effort to renew one's primordial identity as a creature attracted to God. To enter on a pilgrimage is, in some way, to confess one's having strayed from this identity and one's openness to being shown a way back. I wrote earlier that, at the headwaters of the Jordan, my personal pilgrimage began when I scooped the waters in my hand for baptism and experienced their bubbling outside me as awakening a bubbling within. I experienced an awakening of affection that, through the duration of the pilgrimage, I came to understand as the affection of being attracted to God. In the language of Figure 1, the course of my pilgrimage became an extended process of abduction: divinely – and affectively – infused reasoning that draws the self-attracted intellect into the heart and thence into the light of other's hearts and into the fire of God's attractive light itself. In the sub-title of this chapter, I label this an opening to 'The Energetics of Personal Transformation', because 'energetics' refers to the capacity for movement, and I came to understand pilgrimage as opening one's capacity to move indefinitely from self to others: a pilgrim-theologian's words for a journey that opens the soul to our being for others.

Notes

1 This translation of Psalm 42 is by Peter Ochs (from Hebrew).
2 In a study of Coleridge's *Opus Maximum*, Hardy writes,

> The movement of attraction is identified by Coleridge by using a term known in some philosophical circles, chiefly those of modern pragmatism, as 'abduction.' Logically, this is often seen as the postulating of a possible explanation, a 'third' form of reasoning beyond – but Resourcing – induction and deduction. Here in Coleridge, an ancestor of modern pragmatism, however, we find that abduction is 'the being drawn toward the true center' of all, the Logos and the Spirit. A second difference from the usual logical use is that this 'being drawn' incorporates both the ontological and the temporal elements of the created world, including differentiation and continuity, and also the enduring and the progressive, as mutually complementary. A third is that it is applicable both to the individual (as in Aids to Reflection) and also to society (as in On the Constitution of the Church and State), as that which serves 'both for the permanence and the progressive advance of whatever . . . constitute the public weal'. (p. 53)

> In that 'being drawn', human beings are most truly enabled to affirm themselves and the order of all things, as they are illuminated in Reason

and directed in love toward 'all things both great and small, for the dear God who loveth us, He made and loveth all'. This 'abduction' is indeed a maximal insight, a fitting conclusion, both methodological and realistic, to Coleridge's lifelong pursuit of the mutual implication of all things in the Logos and the Spirit. (pp. 51–2. Citations from Daniel W. Hardy, 'Harmony and Mutual Implication in the *Opus Maximum*', in Jeffrey W. Barbeau, ed., *Coleridge's Assertion of Religion: Essays on the Opus Maximum*, Leuven, Paris, Dudley, MA: Peeters, 2006, pp. 33–52)

Hardy is cited in David Ford, 'Daniel Hardy and Scriptural Reasoning: Reflections on his Understanding of Coleridge's *Opus Maximum*', paper delivered for the Cambridge University Inter-faith Programme as part of the conference, 'The Fruitfulness of Dan Hardy's Thought for Scriptural Reasoning' (5–6 June 2008).

3 I do not fully understand what Hardy means by this. At first, I thought he was equating creation and attraction: that we are unable to distinguish between something's being created and its being attracted to the creator. But then he distinguished the two. He said we do not know what it means for something to be created: the most we can say is that to be created is to be dispersed; creation is the dispersion of things, and it is this dispersion that is attractive.

4 Hardy adds: 'Creation is a rich dispersion. This dispersion is what is attractive.' I ask if he would think of creation in terms of the Son's relation to the Father. He answers, 'No, I would rather think of a concentration of relationships rather than discerning the Son and Father.' I ask what kind of concentration this is. He answers, 'We may talk about it as rich dispersion . . . And there is enormous vitality in this – the Christian doctrinal tradition tries to track this too finitely into definite relationships, whereas I would rather speak of concentration and dispersions . . . What marks the concentration is the coming together of the dispersion rather than the Son's movement toward the Father.' He adds that he would speak of the Son's movement only in intimate relation to the Spirit, 'for the Spirit is responsible for the rich multifaceted character of this movement between concentration and dispersion'.

5 I asked Hardy if we can consider God the creator as an extended body. He answered, 'I am not bothered by that.' So we sat together and with profit studied a little of Hasdai Crescas, the medieval Jewish philosopher who was also 'not bothered by that'.

6 In 'Receptive Ecumenism', Hardy writes, 'I have previously offered this account of Coleridge's influence on my diagrams of abductive process:

Here, however, we use it in the sense of being given – or 'being found' by – the primary source and goal of reason, passion and integrity. This use is taken from S. T. Coleridge's Opus Maximum, where ')(' designates continuity in distinction. He describes a 'being drawn toward the true centre' from within the self-referential tendencies of the human self which lead to 'the false and fantastic centre in the opposite direction':

I. Abduction from the Self, as manifesting the being drawn toward the true center, as)(, the self-seeking or tendency to the false and fantastic center in the opposite direction. Attraction ad extra. Appropriative Attraction . . . as)(separative Self-projection, or Volatility.

II. The influx from the Light, with the Spirit[,] as)(by the creaturely: Conjunction: Offspring or realized Poles, Particularization, Contraction as

III. Omneity, Dilation. (Samuel Coleridge, *Opus Maximum*, ed. Thomas McFarland, Princeton: Princeton University Press, 2002, p. 327)

Here we find a distinctive conception of abduction, 'the being drawn toward the true center' of all, the Logos and the Spirit, in distinction from but in continuity with self-seeking or self-reference. Extending this into the social sphere, we find that abduction does not extinguish the self-reference of the activities by which sociopoiesis occurs, but draws them to their 'true center' in the 'influx of Light, with the Spirit'. And, recalling the discussion of arrows just now, the Word and the Spirit attract sociopoiesis and are best seen through their transformative effects on it. They engage fully with socio-poiesis from within, transforming it and all the activities by which it proceeds. Like prophecy and priesthood, by their close engagement with sociopoiesis, the Word and the Spirit transform it, and are to be understood indirectly through their transformative effect on it, neither apart from it nor collapsed into it. As the chart suggests, furthermore, abduction operates not only to draw all human institutions to a higher condition but also to draw them forward to the kingdom of God. (Daniel Hardy, 'Receptive Ecumenism: Learning by Engagement', in Paul Murray, ed., *Receptive Ecumenism and the Call to Catholic Learning: Exploring a Way for Contemporary Ecumenism*, Oxford: Oxford University Press, 2008, pp. 437–8)

7 '"Pascal's Wager" is the name given to an argument due to Blaise Pascal for believing, or for at least taking steps to believe, in God. The name is somewhat misleading, for in a single paragraph of his *Pensées*, Pascal apparently presents at least *three* such arguments, each of which might be called a 'wager' – it is only the final of these, which is traditionally referred to as "Pascal's Wager". We find in it the extraordinary confluence of several important strands of thought: the justification of theism; probability theory and decision theory, used here for almost the first time in history; pragmatism; voluntarism (the thesis that belief is a matter of the will); and the use of the concept of infinity.' (From the online *Stanford Encyclopedia of Philosophy*, http://plato.stanford.edu/entries/pascal-wager/, accessed April 2010.) See Blaise Pascal, *Pascal's Pensées*, trans.W. F. Trotter (1910), Digireads.com Publishing, Stilwell Kansas. For an affirmative account of Pascal's Wager, see Ian Hacking, 'The Logic of Pascal's Wager', *American Philosophical Quarterly* 9/2 (1972), pp. 186–92.

8 To add a few more items of Hardy's vocabulary: 'engagement' is a shorthand term for 'things being implicated with each other' (a surrogate for abduction); 'sympathy' is a shorthand, more pastoral term for rational engagement and thus abduction; 'source of self-enclosure' refers to anything that inhibits one's being attracted.

3

Jericho: Measuring God's Purposes

Narrative

After the headwaters of the Jordan, our group moved south from Nazareth and the Jordan. We made one extended stop before reaching our final goal of Jerusalem: we stopped at Jericho, where I led a eucharistic service. Preparing for the service, I was struck by the significance of Jericho as a relic of the histories and civilizations that preceded the people of Israel in this land. I had read up on the history before the trip, and our guides also peppered the early days of the pilgrimage with the history and geography of the land. So I came to Jericho already with a sense that this place of Israel's first settlement in the land was not a place Israel encountered as a mere barren waste. It was a place that had previously, in a sense, been measured out for God's purposes. I was therefore impressed by the setting of Jericho as if it were a setting pre-prepared for Israel, not a rude, untouched place, but one already nurtured by human history.

These thoughts stimulated me to reflections on what I will call 'being measured for God's purposes'. These reflections became the topic of a sermon I gave during the service. Even though our experiences at Jericho had already served as a stimulus for this, I suggested to the group that the signs of measurement we saw at Jericho would only be fully disclosed when we arrived at Jerusalem. In a comparable way, I devote this chapter to introducing a theological account of measurement, but the deeper source of this account will be displayed only in the next two chapters, when I discuss our arrival in Jerusalem and the great stones that were measured for Jerusalem's Temple there. In Jericho, it had already occurred to me that Jerusalem was a place that had been measured and chosen for God's purposes; and this implied that Israel's movement into the land was not just unguided wandering, but a process that followed some prior activities of estimation, some prior assignation of values, a prior judgement that this place to and through which they were wandering was useful for God's purposes. This thought had never occurred to me before; I had never previously focused on the scriptural accounts of Exodus and Jericho as accounts of measuring and estimating the land for God's purposes. Now I began to reflect on the possibility that such things, including Israel's pilgrimage (and perhaps ours and mine as well), may not just happen haphazardly, but are situated within a pre-estimation.

> God has spoken from his sanctuary:
> 'In triumph I will parcel out Shechem
> and measure off the Valley of Succoth.' (Ps. 108.7, NIV)[1]

This is not to say that what Israel or we do is explicitly pre-planned or predetermined by God. That is distinctly not what I was discovering. I was discovering something neither discretely predetermined nor haphazard in Israel's life and in our own pilgrimage. We could perhaps put it this way: a pilgrimage, or a journeying to the Promised Land, is a kind of wandering, open to the contingencies of space and time, which is at the same time a gradual discovery of purpose. A significant stage of that discovery is to find that we are not wandering on mere barren lands but on places that have already served the purposes of those who came before us, and, moreover, that those places too were built on relics of prior estimations. We must include this entire creation as such an estimation. But we must also bear in mind the indeterminacy present in each estimation, so that what we do in this world leaves room for other ways of enacting what we do – and other ways of making use of what we have done. Searching out those other ways is part of a pilgrimage; the movement of that pilgrimage is to uncover traces of God's purposes through all these possibilities; and the end of the pilgrimage is to have found one's place fully within God's purposes. As I have already suggested, what I am saying here will not become fully clear until the next chapters on Jerusalem, for Jerusalem is a place that displays the ways of God's measurement, while Jericho only introduces us to that topic.

Theological Reflections: Measuring for God's Purposes for Israel and for Christ

In Chapter 2 we examined pilgrimage as a journey to renew one's primordial identity as a creature attracted to God. In this chapter, we gaze not at the pilgrim but at sources of the pilgrim's path: who and what is it that guides the pilgrimage and measures its movement? My theme is that pilgrimage exemplifies a certain pattern of things and invites people to take their place in that pattern and be measured by it: through this measuring a pilgrim acquires the kind of identity we spoke of in Chapter 2. A large part of the work of life is finding our identity in the work of God, and we find this identity by following a certain pattern of things. This is a lifetime process, moving toward our full identity by following this pattern. In the terms introduced in Chapter 2, this means that we are attracted to God and guided to him through this pattern. The whole of life is therefore pilgrimage, being measured by God.

Through a life of pilgrimage, one acquires knowledge of God's purposes, and one discovers that a pilgrim's life is measured by these purposes. To walk in the paths of God is to have one's steps measured by God. This means we are measured by an infinite measure: our paths are not therefore fixed in any way we can imagine, nor do we live in a fixed universe. On one level, God measures us exactly: step here and you die, step there and you live. But on another level, we discover that God's measures are not pre-formed and life's pattern is indefinite. To live as a pilgrim is to move forward through measured steps, every step measured by God.

The meaning of measure

We generally say that to take a measure of something is to estimate its contours. But what occasions our measuring? For the pilgrim, it is to discover plotlessness in one's life and then to seek the plot, which, if found, may be chosen as the measure of one's future movement. Day to day, people rely on fixed measures like copper pots and rulers, appealing to measurements standardized by their societies. Fixed measures of this kind provide a background, a setting for where life's plot is to be enacted, but living out the plot requires a more profound level of measurement: a way to measure one's movement through these settings. Are there fixed standards to measure movement? There is a crucial ambiguity here. Within the language of Newtonian physics, one does indeed measure movement by a standard unit, so that even the speed of light has a standard, $e = mc^2$. Today, however, even in physics we begin to see that not all the movements of the world, or ultimately any of the movements, can be fully measured by finite measures. While Einstein employed Newtonian-like measures to measure the speed of light, he also gave birth to contemporary quantum physics, which employs indefinite measures to measure the movements of sub-atomic particles. The non-finite character of quantum measurement provides a natural science analogue for the non-fixed measure that guides the pilgrim's life. In both cases, we live in a notional universe. But what does this mean?

In quantum physics, the act of measuring the movement of photons, for example, also affects that movement, so that to measure is enter into an actual relation to what is measured. There is no neutral or distant observation here: just as in ethnography, observation is participant-observation, so that the observer (as well as the tools and manner of observation) participate in and influence the activity that is observed. But what of our religious lives and our knowledge of God? Do we measure God? For a life of pilgrimage, to know God is not to observe things 'about' him from some neutral standpoint but to participate in his life in the world. In the vocabulary of Chapter 2, we therefore know God by being attracted into relation with God and into participation in his ways. These ways are his measures. We are drawn into the measure of God in the degree to which we participate in his infinite nature. We recognize that we have been measured by observing *changes* in our actions; to some extent we acquire practices of self-estimation, which are tested and refined as the pilgrim's way continues. In the early stages of a pilgrimage, the pilgrim looks to the self as a source of measure: marking the character and degree of personal transformation as a measure of progress in the pilgrim's movement toward God. Gradually, however, the pilgrim releases the self as such a measure, releasing too, the use of any external standards to measure God – even standards like Jonathan Edwards' 'signs of affection'.[2] By then the pilgrim simply participates in this relation with God, sharing somehow in God's self-measure and losing attraction to any self-measure.

There is however a third party to the pilgrimage. We are all affected by other human beings and by their estimation of us. Beyond measuring ourselves, we find that others measure us in ways that affect our self-measurements. That all means that our self-estimation belongs not only to our inner economy but also to the economy of sociopoiesis, which we defined in the last chapter as the generation and shaping of relations, in this case interpersonal relations in human society. All this applies as well to pilgrims – and to those of us who pursue life as pilgrims – who see that others relate to us as part of their own participation in God. If, therefore, I am attracted to some other – whether Christian or Muslim or Jew – because of my vague sense of being thereby attracted to God, my being attracted to them is also a mark of their participation in God, and they may come to know more of themselves by way of my engagement with them.

These lessons about measurement and sociopoiesis offer us an additional vocabulary for describing what, in Chapter 2, we termed the human capacity to lose attraction to God. We may add that falling out of attraction to God is in part falling out of relation to other persons; we also call this 'narcissism' or preoccupation with self-measurement. Self-measuring is a mark of distance from God and God's measures. Adopting the self as a unit of measure is to occlude measurement by God and attraction to God. It is also to occlude our share in sociopoiesis and the measurements it provides.

Measuring Israel's responsibility on the land

> Then Moses went up from the plains of Moab to Mount Nebo, to the top of Pisgah, which is opposite Jericho, and the LORD showed him the whole land: Gilead as far as Dan, all of Naphtali, the land of Ephraim and Manasseh, all the land of Judah as far as the Western Sea, the Negeb, and the Plain – that is, the valley of Jericho, the city of palm trees – as far as Zoar. The LORD said to him, 'This is the land of which I swore to Abraham, to Isaac, and to Jacob, saying "I will give it to your descendants"; I have let you see it with your eyes, but you shall not cross over there.' (Deut. 34.1–4)

God's measuring out the Holy Land is not neutral measuring; it is part of God's self-measurement. The biblical text's measurement of the greater land of Israel belongs, therefore, to God's infinite measure, rather than to the finite units of any merely human measure. The analogy with quantum measurement applies here as well, suggesting that God's measures are events rather than fixed quantities: events, that is, of God's living relation to the people of Israel and Israel's living relation to the land thus measured. In Deuteronomy 34, Moses is shown the earthly pathway of his people's pilgrimage toward God: the steps they take on this land shall be measured directly by God. The privilege they offer is one of relation to God and therefore of the most profound opportunity and responsibility. Israel shall not say 'this is *my* land', as one would with a land measured by the world's finite measures; they shall say instead 'this is the measure of *my* responsibility'. And so it is with any pilgrimage: a pilgrim's pathway to God is embodied in some worldly movement on some land somewhere in relation to some people; this is the setting of the pilgrim's measurement. At the headwaters of the Jordan, my cognitive understanding of pilgrimage became an affective, embodied one. As we travelled to

Jericho, I believe I was therefore attentive both to the embodied, earthly sense of what it means to inhabit a city on a land *and* to the fact that God meets the pilgrim in this earthly habitation, rather than in some realm of mere cognition. I therefore saw, at once, that Jericho's inhabitants had their God-given place in this city and that Israel had its place, but also that the Bible alerts Israel to the awesome responsibility that comes with its place. I saw that God measures Israel's responsibility in the land and that Scripture discloses that measure. This led me to reflect on how Scripture addresses God's word to the specific community that receives it and with respect to the particular conditions of its life, whether it is the community of Israel, of the Church or of the Ummah.

Measuring the Church: Scripture as measure

Like a person, a community may be said to undertake a pilgrimage to God, seeking to find its identity in God. If, following Coleridge, we locate the primordial identities of all creaturely life in God the creator, then we may also name each community's pilgrimage a renewal of identity. Like a person, a community begins such a path of renewal by acknowledging its having strayed from God's way and declaring its openness to leave the confines of self-attraction and seek relations with others once again:[3] relations with God but also with other communities and with individuals who have become 'other' to the community. Through its movement toward such others, the community renews what we may call its inner or constitutive sociopoiesis and its place in the sociopoiesis of all humanity and all creation. For Christians, Jews and Muslims, the first guide and measure of such movement is Scripture. Scripture narrates each community's birth in historical time, its primordial activities of identity formation and its prototypical acts of confession, pilgrimage and renewal. Scripture thereby displays God's measure – the divine word – in a way that directly addresses the community's need for guidance in renewing its sociopoiesis. In the language of Scripture, this measure often appears as the 'law' or 'time' or the One who 'renews the covenant':

> These are the words of the covenant that the LORD commanded Moses to make with the Israelites in the land of Moab, in addi-

tion to the covenant that he had made with them at Horeb. (Deut. 29.1)[4]

Joshua gathered all the tribes of Israel to Shechem, and summoned the elders, the heads, the judges, and the officers of Israel; and they presented themselves before God . . . So Joshua made a covenant with the people that day, and made statutes and ordinances for them at Shechem. (Josh. 24.1, 25)

God finds fault with them when he says: 'The days are surely coming, says the Lord, when I will establish a new covenant with the house of Israel and with the house of Judah.' (Heb. 8.8)

Scripture is the source and measure of a community's turning to a path of pilgrimage and healing. Using a term that has only recently become meaningful to me, I would say that Scripture enables the healing powers deep within a pilgrim (whether a community or person) to 'granulate'. Recovering from a medical treatment recently, I learned that 'granulation' refers to the body's capacity to generate new connective tissue from deep within the flesh, just underneath the diseased tissue that lies above it. This is a hopeful sign, because it shows how the rebuilding of tissue is possible from within the deepest parts of the human body. I would extend the metaphor to the capacity of societies and persons to be regenerated from deep within themselves. Communities and individual persons do lose their way and suffer 'disease' – but their cure emerges from deep within them: from 'underneath' the disease. By analogy, Scripture does not deliver its healing from outside the pilgrim, but by drawing out the capacity of attraction that lies deep within. The ultimate terrain of human redemption lies deep within us. The Scripture that delivers God's measure is not therefore all laid out for us on the surface. Scripture heals through the way that we are 'scriptured', or drawn into a process of re-generation that imitates the very process that generates our Scriptures. In the gospel, we see people following Jesus as he wanders around Palestine; they refind their identities as, following him, they come to participate in the process that generates gospel.

Measuring the Church: The Eucharist as measure

The Church is born in the process that generates our gospel. In the pilgrimage of the Church, the Kingdom is one measure of God's purposes, not as a set of rules, but as showing the end of the journey: a fully embodied Sabbath and the most intimate relation with God, with all humans and all creation. It is Scripture, again, that discloses the Kingdom and the fullness of all God's purposes. Scripture as a whole measures the Church, but the defining measure of the Church is the sacrament of the Eucharist. To explain this I shall return to the analogy we drew between quantum physics and the ecclesiology I am developing here. We noted that while Newtonian physics identified fixed measures of physical movement, quantum measurement is not fixed, because it must take into account the conditions of measurement: the effect any instruments of measure have on the sub-atomic particle being measured. Analogously, the Church is not measured by any fixed standard, because the Church is embodied in its practices and its practices embody a living relationship among its members and the triune persons of God. The measure of the Church lies within this relationship and is embodied within church practices. Eucharist names the element of church practice that most clearly typifies the whole: the name *per se* of God's redemptive presence in the life of the Church. Eucharist is the practical activity which founds church society: 'The Lord's (or "Last") Supper' – in which Christians share in the life, death and resurrection of Jesus Christ – is the pure primal event by which righteousness was constituted in Jesus' time, and it is fully recalled each time it is re-enacted.

> But there is a further depth of meaning standing behind that. The 'original' event, the Last Supper, is also a memorial of other primal events by which there is a world in which there is redemption. Whenever there is mention of 'God making the world and loving creation' or of the circumstances into which Jesus came for our salvation . . . there are references to the primal event of creation, to its declaration as 'good' by the triune God, and to the entire history of God with those whom he creates and with whom he covenants.[5]

The most direct way to observe how the Eucharist guides the society of the Church is not to study doctrine, but to attend to the strictly local context of the performance of Eucharist. 'It faces those present, within their particular circumstances, with themes and counter-themes of human existence, and stimulates them to a new course of social life – a new enactment of meaning that approximates to goodness in their place.'[6] Eucharist measures the Church by measuring the progress of each member's pilgrimage to God within the sociopoiesis of a given church and in the sociopoiesis that gathers all churches and all creatures in God's creation.

Measurement and abduction

If we are unaccustomed to applying the notion of 'measurement' to our lives in the Church, it may be a sign of our modern habit of disassociating the life of the Church from the activities of the material world studied by natural scientists.[7] This habit is another symptom of tendencies in the modern Church to turn inward, toward self-reference rather than toward others. This 'turning in' is reinforced by an opposing tendency in the modern natural and social sciences: to turn 'outward', not in the sense of engaging the other in relationship, but in the sense of measuring the outside worlds of nature and society by fixed and therefore purportedly 'objective' measures. Trusting that modern science understands the outer world correctly, modern humanists as well as theologians may direct their gaze inward to avoid losing their identities altogether in a world of fixed measures.

However, tendencies in more recent science, from interpretive anthropology to quantum physics, suggest a much stronger continuity between the role of the observer in the sciences and of the interpreter in the humanities and the theologian's practices of reading. While measures will be more defined on one side of the continuum than the other, both sides now tend to recognize the relational character of much of what we know. Within the precincts of the Church, this means we need no longer associate the 'externals' of religious practice with fixed measures. Nothing that God has spoken into being, neither his creatures nor his commandments, appears to us fully formed or fixed in character and dimension; nor are these beings fully formed and fixed by the processes and relations through which we know them. Neither fully defined nor undefined in themselves, all these things that God 'spoke' achieve their full identities through all the relations that bind them to all of creation. This is the epistemological meaning of sociopoiesis as a primordial feature of the created world.

The notion of measurement is problematic only in its modern usage, when it is applied only to an 'outer' rather than 'inner' world and only with respect to fixed units of measure. Within this ecclesiology, however, it is applied to our source of information about any kind of end-directed behaviour, in particular about how ends (norms, ideals, guidelines or identities) are embodied in practice. In these terms, fixed measurement is indeed one kind of measurement, applied to certain dimensions of ourselves and of the world, but, when applied to other dimensions, units of measure will be more or less undefined or defined only with respect to complex and variable relations. It is in the latter sense that we speak of the Eucharist as a measure of the Church. To clarify how the Eucharist measures, it is best to revisit the notion of abduction introduced in Chapter 2.

There, abduction was characterized as 'our capacity to turn away from self-engagement back to our primordial attraction to others and to God', and we added that 'abduction opens our capacity to answer questions that cannot otherwise be answered', leading us both cognitively and affectively 'beyond our self-understanding and our customary practices . . . into ever-new relations to the other' and to God. Applying the terms of this chapter, we may add that abduction names each pilgrim's capacity to glimpse the standard of measure that defines his or her pilgrimage. No longer trusting the adequacy of existing forms of measurement, the pilgrim seeks God's measure, alone. For Coleridge, this seeking is a continual sense, born of life in the Church: there is yet a higher measure to be found. Like an attractive force, this sense pushes the pilgrim forward, in mind and affection, to the divine. It is what Coleridge called the 'Logos in Spirit' – the form of the Logos and the energy of the Spirit – which draws the person in full integrity back to God's embrace.[8] It is what, in Chapter 2, was described as the pilgrim's turning back to the primordial source of attraction; in this sense, because this source is present in every creature of God, every creature is a potential pilgrim. Abduction is therefore potentially present in every cognition and every affection, since every one is a consequence of the Creator's 'I am' present in each creaturely movement.[9] If so, why do we not sense every cognition and affection as an opening toward God?

The problem is simply that somehow, in our world, something interferes with what should be a natural attraction. One name for this obstruction is the sheer multiplicity of things placed before us. I cannot say whether it is part of the human condition or only of our society that, as creatures of sensibility, we cannot resist being pulled away from the depths of things, dispersed. To the degree that this is part of our human condition, I call this 'extensity'. Like the movement of creation itself, dispersing all things away from their origin, our powers of being attracted are drawn away from their source into the multiplicity of things, and this counter-attraction is in tension with our inner attraction to God. Extensity is necessary to our creaturely condition, so that we may carry out God's command to 'go forth' and to engage all his creatures; but this spreading out also makes it more difficult for us to maintain our unity with God. Drawn outward as we should be, we are then in danger of losing our sense of God's presence within us: we leave the garden. We have two natures: we are distributed human beings, which means that we are drawn to look around at all things; and we are primordially attracted to the God within. The goal for us is to keep these two natures in balance. Ultimately this balance is guided and measured by the attraction that turns us within, but that guides us to apply this measure without as well. Beyond these inner tensions in our human nature, we are also shaped today by a cultural tendency to over-balance our attraction to what lies without: our eyes are cast all about with no place for them to rest. Capitalism is a major source of this cultur-ally induced extensity. It overweighs the distributed character of things, and the tendency magnifies itself so that what is distrib-uted re-distributes, and we risk forgetting what lies within rather than without. We are made to think that it is normal for things to ramify more and more without rest or centre.

Amid such challenges, how is our primordial attraction reawakened? If abduction names the process that turns us back toward our origin, then what stimulates abduction? The name I use for this stimulus is 'rational frustration'. Whatever its source (that much we cannot account for), rational frustration arises as a sense that we are not doing what we ought to do: in this case, a sense that this extreme extensity goes against our inner natures. This sense pushes us to reason, specifically to look within our experience for signs of something that might counter this troublesome tendency: searching for patterns of order or unity. But rational frustration stops there: the most it can do is re-direct our attention to something apparently free of this wayward tendency. There are hazards here as well, since we may find ourselves attracted to this single moment of reasoning, rather than moving through to the attraction we originally sought. Perhaps some self-contained projects in philosophy and metaphysics are products of this midway attraction: projects that risk turning reason into an idol rather than an instrument of divine service.

Rational frustration works successfully when it turns our attention to observe and then participate in patterns of order and unity that are not simply human constructs but windows to primordial patterns of attraction. This activity usually operates in two ways simultaneously. There is an outer joy in sensing patterns of order that appear in the cosmos: as the psalmist declares, 'The heavens are telling the glory of God; and the firmament proclaims his handiwork'[10] (these are often observations of unity in multiplicity); and at the same time there is an inner sign, a joyful integrity that emerges within the soul while one turns to look out at the patterns. The joining of these outer and inner activities is what we call abduction. We may distinguish three modes and levels of abduction:

- *Abduction 1: encyclopedic abduction, or observing cosmological unity*
  This is the activity of seeing patterns in worldly multiplicity. Coleridge, for example, reasoned his way through the entire *Encyclopedia Metropolitiana* to disclose its unity. This pattern of reasoning is analogous to the cosmological argument in Thomas Aquinas.[11]

- *Abduction 2: Inner abduction, or discovering personal integrity*
  This is the activity of discovering or rediscovering one's personal integrity. For Coleridge, this is the strong moral impulse (and Coleridge is close to Kant in this way): it concerns actively embracing the good as a prime motive; a view that runs counter to doctrines of passive grace. This active embrace engages one with the Spirit Logos.

- *Abduction 3: Relational abduction*
  It is difficult to name this activity, since our vocabularies tend to name any relation with respect to either its inner or outside poles, and this activity belongs to both. Acknowledging this difficulty, we might identify this abduction as that which integrates these two dimensions:

  o *3a) Abduction as the integration of person and pattern, or inner integrity and the created order.* This is the activity through which the outer and inner abductions are integrated.
  o *3b) Abduction as primary attraction.* This is the activity that displays the measure of measures. The activity of integrating outer and inner is Attraction itself.

Eucharistic abduction

To refer to the Eucharist as a measure of the Church, therefore, is to refer to its sacramental practice as an activity that may foster *relational abduction.* Guided by scriptural accounts of the Last Supper, eucharistic practice integrates the unity of the worldly body (the body of the human being and the body of the empirical Church) with the unity of the inner spirit (the integrity of the person and of the Church in the Spirit Logos). Enacting this relational abduction displays the ecclesial measure of measures, and this *is divine attraction.* To enact the measure of measures is to bring its intensity into the extensity of the worldly Church. *This is the activity of assembling all that needs to be assembled to promote the fullness of human society. This is ecclesiology. And the purpose of this book is right here: to talk about the activity through which we measure the measures. This is the activity of church formation and scriptural enactment; it is the activity, at once, of Eucharist, Scripture and ecclesiology.*

Eucharistic abduction is a means of educating the pilgrim's desires in service to the Church. Enacting this education is to walk a path of church formation and scriptural enactment: each step on the path is an action taken and a judgement made according to the measure of measures. Such judgements are total, integrating all dimensions of personal being – cognitive and affective – and they are relational, extending the person to others in the world simultaneously as they attract the person inward to God. Each step draws the pilgrim into sociopoiesis and extends sociopoiesis into this region where the pilgrim walks: the pilgrimage is utterly social, while also utterly worldly and utterly sacramental.

Notes

1 In the Masoretic canon, this is Psalm 108.8. The Hebrew term for 'to measure' is למדוד (*limdod*); 'a measure' (and also 'a step') is מידה (*midah*). In the Septuagint Greek the root is *metro* (μέτρο), 'measure'.

2 Jonathan Edwards, *A Treatise Concerning Religious Affections in Three Parts*. See Jonathan Edwards, *The Works of Jonathan Edwards, Vol. 2: Religious Affections*, ed. John E. Smith, New Haven: Yale University Press, 2009.

3 See Chapter 2, pp. 49–53.

4 Deuteronomy 28.69 in the Masoretic canon.

5 Daniel W. Hardy, *Finding the Church: The Dynamic Truth of Anglicanism* (London: SCM Press, 2001), p. 248.

6 Hardy, *Finding the Church*, p. 247. Hardy gathers a maximal range of activities under the term 'Eucharist': from the way congregants of a particular church gather to receive bread and wine as the body and blood of Christ, to the consequences of this gathering in the continuing life of the congregation and its members (including consequences in the lives of those whom they encounter outside their church), to the life of God – incarnate in this universe, in humanity, in the body of Christ –, to the life of God's Word in Scripture as well as sacrament, to the material and social lives of those who became congregants of this church and joined its communion.

7 This is one focus of Hardy's *God's Ways with the World* (Edinburgh: T & T Clark, 1996).

8 In *Finding the Church*, Hardy writes,

[For Coleridge,] knowledge finds its proper place only when it embraces moral goodness (when it is 'sub-ordinated' to the Good). It is the ordering of the two in relation to each other, within the constitution provided by creation and by reference to God, which occurs when truth is pursued 'for the sake of THE TRUE,' when the search for truth is oriented to the

One in whom truth is fully good, God. Still more simply, 'Truth + Good = Wisdom,' where wisdom is also holiness. (p. 46)

Hardy then cites Coleridge's account of holy wisdom:

[T]he Good (the self-originating Father) + the Logos (or the Truth or the true Light) = σοφία, the Wisdom – for such was the most ancient appellative of the Holy Ghost . . .' (S. T. Coleridge, *Shorter Works and Fragments*, vol. I, ed. H. J. Jackson and J. R. de J. Jackson, London: Routledge, 1995, p. 448)

See also Samuel Taylor Coleridge, *Aids to Reflection and the Confessions of an Inquiring Spirit*, Whitefish, MT: Kessinger, 2004, pp. 44, 46. But note also Hardy's cautions about Coleridge's transcendentalism: *God's Ways*, pp. 189–93.

9 Hardy argues that, unlike Coleridge, Peirce applies the term 'abduction' to humanly generated hypotheses as well as to those insights that arise exclusively through divine attraction. While I agree with Hardy, I would add that Peirce measures the ultimate truth of the former through evidences of the latter and that, for Peirce, God is present directly in every experience.

10 Psalm 19.1.

11 For illustrations of Hardy's cosmological abductions, see *God's Ways*: with respect to physics, for example, see pp. 120–30, 155–7, 256–7. Cf. Charles Peirce, 'A Neglected Argument for the Reality of God', *Hibbert Journal* 7/1 (1908), pp. 90–112; repr. in Charles Peirce, *Collected Papers of Charles Sanders Peirce*, vol. 6, eds. Charles Hartshorne and Paul Weiss, Cambridge, MA: Harvard University Press, 1935, vol. 6, par. 452–85.

4
Jerusalem: Jesus' Steps, Measuring the Church

Narrative

Jerusalem was on my mind when I spoke in Jericho about God's measuring the land. If Jerusalem was *the* place measured and chosen for God's purposes and if the Holy Land was measured out in anticipation of that, then the signs of measurement we saw at Jericho would only be fully disclosed in Jerusalem. The first sign of this disclosure came just as we entered Jerusalem. Our entire pilgrimage was scheduled so that we would arrive at St George's Cathedral in time to attend the installation of the new Anglican Bishop of Jerusalem.[1] Shortly after his consecration, I became aware of a pillar of light appearing in front of the church: a blazing pillar whose light was the most intense possible. The light drew me to it, as if it were the centre of what is attractive: the attractiveness of the Lord. After this first manifestation, experiences of light reappeared to me throughout our time in Jerusalem. Since my youth I have experienced manifestations of light: not as an inner light, but an outer light, emerging primarily from and around the people I am speaking with. The light that gradually dominated my experiences in Jerusalem was light of this same kind, but with a frequency and intensity that I had never experienced before. Toward the end of our visit to Jerusalem, this manifestation began to assume its own importance, so that it was in a sense self-presenting, self-interpreting; and it became increasingly intensive as time went on, denser, more focused and persisting for longer durations of time.

The experience at St George's was of a shaft of light within the environment of the church. The shaft was like a 'twister' of light, a column that moved into different configurations in different directions. It was a strange experience: I felt I could reach out and gather the light in. I did that, and it felt very immediate; it is difficult to describe, but I felt that I was vividly inside the light, participating in it, simultaneously gathering it in and being gathered into it, and finding in this place a feeling of blessedness, the kind one might feel after a long period of contemplation. It was a joy, a feeling that things had fallen into place. It was a total reorientation, where God was visible everywhere in the light: it was the intensity of the Lord, made visible in and by the Church universal, located that particular day in St George's.

Retrospectively, that first experience of a pillar of light seems like a consummation of what I was yet to see. But it was also like an embodied answer to a question that has been on my mind for some time. Running back over a few years, I have been deeply interested in the question of the infinitely intense identity of the Lord. I have tended to articulate my findings through words and ideas, but, in Jerusalem, the reality of this intense identity was embedded in a visual experience of a pillar of light, making graphic what was otherwise only conceptual. The light magnified the meaning of God's infinite identity for me hugely. I could now answer: 'What is this identity?' It is of the intensity of light: light of an intensity that overreaches all things, so that there is nothing that could stand outside of it. It is not an inner light, but a light that is manifested outside and may then be remembered within. The colour of this light may be white or golden at times, but I assume it is a colour that has no apparent character until it is refracted by some elements of our atmosphere, our world, and made visible through the refraction.[2] In this sense, one cannot call the visible light 'pure', since it is in a sense mediated by the way things appear in this world; I experienced it increasingly as light shining upon things, coming down and suffusing them so that the light is as if it is deep within those things. The light draws my attention towards them: at first, perhaps, I am drawn to them for some other reason, but as I gaze on them I begin to see that what attracts me is not the thing in itself but the light that shines on them and then, gradually, only the light itself. This light came to define my experience of Israel as a whole.

After the light at St George's Cathedral, I gradually came to experience light shining off the stones of Jerusalem, and I began to meditate on Jesus who stepped on those stones. I reflected how, as he walked the streets of Jerusalem and all the land of Palestine, Jesus' steps measured God's presence in the Holy Land. In my memory, there was always that experience of the light together with my thoughts on the infinite identity of the Lord, and there was a return to the sense of God's measuring the land. At Jericho, it was the God of Israel measuring the whole land and then the city of Jerusalem for his purposes: in Jerusalem, it was Jesus' measuring each step of the city by the steps he took through it; then it was Jesus' measuring the people of the land by the way he walked towards and with (and then stood by) each one.

It was unfortunate that the tour did not discuss the politics of Jericho on the West Bank; it ignored that. In this sense, I felt somewhat apart from the tour as a whole, having (as it seemed at times, at least) a somewhat different experience, particularly in relation to the land and how people live on the land. I realized that the land is measured and that to live on it is to *be* measured. At the eucharistic service at Jericho, I spoke to this theme and said that we needed to attend to Jericho as a physical, geographical and historical place, but this was not taken up, so my thoughts on measurement remained private, as was an emerging sense of light.

Our first days in Jerusalem were set in the ambience, the location and the circumstance of a new step in the formation of the Church: the replacement of one bishop by another. For me the occasion was accompanied by something even greater than the usual pomp and circumstance that attends a consecration. Reflecting on how the work of two Anglican bishops might address the challenging theopolitics of Jerusalem, I arrived at a new stage in my own understanding of church formation. The Holy Land, over which we crossed, was home to a beleaguered Palestinian community, but one hoped that something coming out of Jerusalem itself would ameliorate the situation. Indeed, the Archbishop of the Province of Jerusalem and the Middle East[3] is a man of great gentleness and peace, whose friendly connections with the Muslims in Cairo are remarkable, including a warm friendship with the grand mufti of Egypt. He seeks to build up the best kind of relations, someone whose efforts might become an example to others, and the new Bishop of Jerusalem seems, indeed, to share these traits. After having seen so many of the problems of the church in Palestine, I therefore saw great hope in the presence of both these church leaders: that, through warmth of human relation and through a kind of inter-religious pastoral embrace, they would open new long-term possibilities for relations among Christians and Muslims and hopefully Jews as well.

Ruminating on the theopolitics of the church in the Middle East, I observed a series of reasons why what is so helpful inside the Anglican Church may make the Anglican Church a possible source of hope throughout the Middle East. At best, Anglicans try not to be so arrogant as to assume they are always right: we try to remember, instead, that we are only one part of the total Church and therefore have only part of the answers. Our way is to take things as we find them and then work in relation to them. In place of triumphal declarations of the truth, we – at our best – value moderation and participation, a quality of embrace that gathers people actually to work with each other on the ground. These values are associated with a willingness to live within the historical situations in which the Church finds itself, and to wait for change to come through the long term of history.

This willingness suggests a profound sense of the purposes of the divine and a prayerful search for the divine presence that would truly refresh the places we inhabit, drawing us forward. This is an openness to what we may call *temporal abduction*, which means allowing our imaginations to be drawn forward by divine attraction: an ongoing process of envisioning and re-envisioning, so that we are stretched forward by the divine purposes. This openness has its source in something very deep within Anglicanism. In Richard Hooker's terms, it is to emphasize the fullness of God within the divine purposes, which is to allow oneself to be moved forward by God: moved forward in imagination, in mode of behaviour, in one's mode of reasoning and in one's sociality. Temporal abduction is a temporal movement of the Spirit: an abduction that grabs you into the spirit's wind and pulls you along in the direction of the divine movement: 'The spirit blows where it chooses; you hear the sound of it, but you don't know where it comes from or where it is going.' (John 3.8). I hope we may all be enriched by this spirit-movement, which is also a moving forward of hope.

This is the source of my hope for Israel–Palestine. In the spirit moving forward I see a theopolitical force that may move not only the church of the Middle East but its politics. This is the hope I saw (and see) in my experience of the pillar of light by St George's Cathedral: that experiencing this light is being moved in and by the Spirit and that the Spirit opens possibilities for theopolitical outreach to *all* the human beings in this troubled area. The Anglican Church has a heritage of attending to this aspect of the Spirit arising in history. This heritage is not well recognized today, but it merits close attention. One of the strengths of Anglicanism is its capacity to observe the Spirit moving in history and politics and to recognize that this is a spirit that all peoples can see in their own ways. This spirit is a source of hope for what all peoples in this land and throughout the Middle East might see if they were not blinded by their own agendas. Materialism, self-interest and particularism keep people from seeing this spirit in Jerusalem, as if things have to be set in stone for them to have any value at all, but these same stones are moved by the Spirit: made visible in the light I saw first at St George's and then over all the stones of the city.

Bringing the hope of the Spirit to every place in which it touches down, temporal abduction offers a missiology, since it makes visible how the Church moves through other places of the world, giving witness to the movement of the Spirit. The purpose of this missiology is witness, not conversion, since its witness is to help people see, by way of what the Anglican Church has observed in history, how each people may find the Spirit there in its own place. This missiology belongs to an ecclesiology of opening and embrace rather than of conquest and triumph.

Temporal abduction is hugely expansive in two ways: in its capacity to regenerate and in its temporal thrust, drawing us forward into a fuller relation with the divine. This movement is eschatological in a very full sense. It emerges underneath conditions of extreme distress, like the conditions now in Israel–Palestine. From out of the very thicket of trouble, there is an incredible growth of unexpected hope and promise: the renewed possibility of life that leads us to exclaim, 'We haven't seen anything yet!' It comes at first as a very slow granulation of new relations, processes and institutions of sociopoiesis: starting directly underneath those that are most troubled and dis-eased. The movement is not individualized but emerges as a renewed social ecology: since the rebuilding moves across the whole rather than from out of individual parts, it cannot be measured by instruments formed out of separate parts (like standard rulers that measure length by the standard of a single part, such as an inch or a centimetre). Temporal abduction is measured only by the whole, which means only by the ultimate measures that God brings down to earth. The Church is such a measure and Scripture is another measure: the word 'canon', in fact (often used to characterize an authorized collection of sacred books), is a Middle English term derived from roots that suggest 'measurement': the Latin *canonicus*, and the Greek κανωνικος, 'relating to a rule'. A 'canon' is a rule or body of principles, derivatively a collection of texts that define the rule. And, finally, the Eucharist is an ultimate measure: the source and rule of all sociopoiesis embodied in our midst.

Divine measurement is not coercive. For Christians this is illustrated in the fact that Jesus wanders through Palestine. He does not have coercive intent in walking around the Holy Land. He is measuring it, but not in the sense that he is saying 'Here I am! This is what to do and how to do it. Now, move on.' It is much gentler than that. It is a pulse of healing that does not overwhelm people but finds them where they are, engages them, opens breathing space for them and then draws them forward. God's measure comes with a kind of benevolent, rolling effect.

Theological Reflection: Theopolitics and Measurement

Jesus walks through the land

[A]fter getting into a boat [Jesus] crossed the water and came to his own town

As Jesus was walking along, he saw a man called Matthew sitting at the tax booth . . .

While he was saying these things to them, suddenly a leader of the synagogue came in and knelt before him, saying, 'My daughter has just died; but come and lay your hand on her, and she will live.' And Jesus got up and followed him, with his disciples. Then suddenly a woman who had been suffering from haemorrhages for twelve years came up behind him and touched the fringe of his cloak, for she said to herself, 'If I only touch his cloak, I will be made well.' Jesus turned, and seeing her he said, 'Take heart, daughter; your faith has made you well.' And instantly the woman was made well. When Jesus came to the leader's house and saw the flute-players and the crowd making a commotion, he said, 'Go away; for the girl is not dead but sleeping.' And they laughed at him. But when the crowd had been put outside, he went in and took her by the hand, and the girl got up. And the report of this spread throughout that district.

As Jesus went on from there, two blind men followed him, crying loudly, 'Have mercy on us, Son of David!'

Then Jesus went about all the cities and villages, teaching in their synagogues, and proclaiming the good news of the king-dom, and curing every disease and every sickness. When he saw the crowds, he had compassion for them, because they were harassed and helpless, like sheep without a shepherd. Then he said to his disciples, 'The harvest is plentiful, but the labourers are few; therefore ask the Lord of the harvest to send out labourers into his harvest.' (Matthew 9)

Consider how Jesus walked the land in this story: he stepped into a boat and crossed into the town; and he went from there and saw a tax collector. Then a ruler came, then a woman who was bleeding. Then he went from there . . . He went through all the towns and villages, preaching, teaching and healing. Thinking about this chapter, I awoke one night with a strong sense of the power of Jesus' walking. It wasn't theory; it wasn't theology or doctrine. He was walking, step by step through the land, and after every set of steps he met someone, stood by someone, one to one, and in some way he touched and healed each one. Perhaps we have underestimated the power of this one-to-one healing. Perhaps the possibility of real healing for us and for this land is greater than we have allowed. Perhaps there is reason for more theopolitical hope than we have imagined. God's presence is outworking among us in a low-key way, and we may not have been looking for so modest a way: as simple as the quality of Jesus' walking, the way people respond to him, the way he is present to them and the way they are deeply healed.

I awoke that night with a strong sense that the Gospels are under-read, in the sense that the people are looking beyond what the narrative says, beyond the specific quality of what is happening between Jesus and those around them. People may say back to me, 'No, you are under-reading, because you don't fill your reading with doctrinal assertion.' But to my way of thinking, that would be to over-read. To read about Jesus' walking is to observe the healing that comes out in Jesus' contact with the people: healing that comes in a low-key way, unexpected – almost unnoticed – like the gradual thickening of once-wounded tissue as it heals. Jesus' healing is unexpected because he comes in the manner of a fellow human but heals as God, bringing not only physical healing, but transformation at every level of the inner being.

The woman who bleeds touches Jesus' cloak: this is a powerful example of how Jesus' healing does not come 'instantaneously' as it may appear (as if it were a matter of mere externality), but slowly, as something Jesus has offered her enters into the depths of *who she is*, working at the core of her being. She becomes aware that something has shifted very deep within her: some deep amelioration ingrained with her being. When I awoke that night, I knew of that kind of healing: a powerful presence that goes down to the depths, surfaces slowly and attracts a kind of healing.

Perhaps the only outer evidence of this is a calm transformation. This can be understood in everyday terms, but not through overly rationalized analysis. My outer illness provides the occasion for an unexpected healing of a much deeper kind and this helps me understand what may happen when Jesus visits and heals those who come to him with all varieties of illness. They sense that a remarkable presence is in front of them and that some gradual change is working deep within them. This experience could not be captured in the conceptually finite terms of messianic theology or doctrine. Introducing theological concepts may in fact obstruct the inner movement that was opened by Jesus' presence; the concepts are mere externals, but the movement is of a deeply inner healing, a granulation in the inner tissue of their being. This movement will continue as long as the people who have met Jesus allow it to continue by letting it enter as fully as possible into every feature of their daily lives.

Healing and the birth of inner measure

I spoke in Jericho of how the God of Israel measures the land. But how does God measure the people who live on the land? In Jerusalem, I encountered Jesus walking through the city, but his walking does not appear at first to answer the question, how does God measure the people? Jesus' walking seems too ordinary, too understated, too human to speak to the enormous questions of divine measurement. Furthermore, Jesus' walking has to do with healing just one person at a time. But what would healing have to do with measurement and how, on a divine scale, could healing work just one person at a time, face to face?

Perhaps it would be helpful at this point to draw several of the previous discussions together and, in the process, to bring some of my earlier abstract conclusions down to earth, where both healing and measurement take place. In the previous chapter, I introduced the notion of Eucharist as measure of the Church and how it measures the Church by 'measuring the progress of each member's pilgrimage to God within the sociopoiesis of a given church and in the sociopoiesis that gathers all churches and all creatures in God's creation'. I suggested that Coleridge's notion of 'abduction' would help us see more clearly how each individual's pilgrimage could be measured. I characterized 'abduction' as 'our capacity to turn away from self-engagement back to our primordial attraction to others and to God'. This capacity accompanies every act by every one of God's creatures; yet 'somehow, in our world, something interferes with what should be a natural attraction', something like the sheer multiplicity of things, or an imbalance between our two creaturely tendencies to enter the world (extensity) and to remain focused on God (intensity).

The question is, then, how can we return home to God and bring others with us? Borrowing Coleridge's terms again, I suggested that the stimulus to return is 'rational frustration': 'a sense that we are not doing what we ought to do . . . that pushes us to reason, specifically to look within our experience for signs of something that might counter this troublesome tendency'. Rational frustration stops there, however: 'the most it can do is re-direct our attention . . . to observe and then participate in patterns of order and unity that are not simply human constructs but windows to primordial patterns of attraction'. I spoke of an 'outer joy in sensing patterns of order that appear in the cosmos' and 'an inner sign, a joyful integrity that emerges within the soul while one turns to look out at the patterns. The joining of these outer and inner activities is what we call abduction.' I mentioned three phases of abduction: observing cosmological unity, discovering personal integrity and 'relational abduction, integrating inner integrity and the created order and thereby recovering our primordial attraction to God within the creation'.[4] Finally, I identified the Eucharist as a measure of the Church – and thus *a measure of measures* – because its sacramental practice fosters *relational abduction*: '. . . assembling all that needs to be assembled to promote the fullness of human society'. *I concluded that this activity of measuring the measures is ecclesiology, the topic of this book.* 'Eucharistic abduction is a means of educating the pilgrim's desires in service to the Church. Enacting this education is to walk a path of church formation and scriptural enactment.'

This ecclesiology is an account of how each creature, and each

1. At the Headwaters of the Jordan

2. Security wall on the road to Jericho

3. Jerusalem overlook: The old city

4. Light on the temple walls

5. The 'Dominus Flevit' Chapel (the site where 'the Lord wept over Jerusalem')

6. Marc Chagall's 'The Tribe Simeon' window at the Hadassah Hospital Synagogue

7. *Emerging from the tunnel under the Wailing Wall*

8. *The Monastery of the Divine Fire at Mt. Sinai*

*9. Daniel W. Hardy,
Birmingham University,
England 1983*

*10. Daniel W. Hardy, Van Mildert
Professor of Theology, Durham
University, England, 1987*

11. Daniel W. Hardy, Cape Cod

12. Twin Lakes, Salisbury, Connecticut, USA

13. The Hardy family: Chris, Deborah (Ford), Daniel, Perrin, Jen and Dan (Jr), Cambridge, England 2007

14. Daniel W. Hardy, Deborah Hardy Ford, Peter Ochs and David Ford, Twin Lakes, Salisbury, Connecticut, USA, 2007

15. Daniel W. Hardy
9 November 1930 – 15 November 2007

community of creatures, recovers its primordial attraction to each other and to God. As the body of Christ, the Church is at once the measure and the place and time of this recovery, and each empirical church embodies the measure in its historical place and time. Over a lifetime, I have examined the concrete practices of the Anglican Church and churches as prototypes of this embodiment.[5] In this book, I speak only out of these prototypes but for the sake of a potentially more general account. The prototype for this more general account is the Gospel narrative of Jesus' walking. I see his walking as the measure of measures, and I see the land of Israel–Palestine as the historical place and time of his walking. Ecclesiology is embodied: in Jesus' walking.

Another step is to read the illness or dis-ease of each person who comes to Jesus as analogous to what I termed (more abstractly) the conditions of obstruction that lead us to rational frustration. This dis-ease not only obstructs full bodily life but also tends to deflect attention away from the person's primordial attractions and to this dis-eased body instead. During our pilgrimage, the worldly dis-ease that drew most of my attention was the dis-ease of Palestinian life on the soil of the Holy Land and of relations among Israelis and Palestinians. I was as troubled by the strife and the bodily discomforts among these peoples as I was by the fact that, unhealed, these discomforts seemed to draw all attention away from each person's and each people's primordial attractions and their deepest sources of value and integrity. Consider what those who need healing may feel when they see this stranger, Jesus, coming along ... They must be puzzled: who is it who wanders around freely like this, engaging whomever he meets? His presence prompts something in them, but what? This doesn't fit their expectation of what healing and a healer looks like.

Yet another step is to read the directness and simplicity of Jesus' walking-healing as a wholly embodied prototype of the measure of measures that I previously characterized (conceptually) as 'relational abduction' and, sacramentally, as eucharistic performance. Here, in the land of Israel–Palestine, where the 'congregation' numbers Palestinians and Israelis, the wholly embodied question is to ask what we should expect 'relational abduction' to look like among these people. According to what has been suggested in this chapter, it would look like Jesus' walking and healing: simple, direct, non-conceptual and non-grandiose, no grand political or theopolitical scheme, no grand pronouncements. Speaking from out of the Church (still), we cannot say how Israelis and Palestinians would conceive of and anticipate such healing if they sought it. We can, however, speak of how, anticipating Jesus' walking, we in the Church would act on this soil. This wandering Jesus shows us what it means to care for the Church and what it means for the Church to care for its members. We learn from Jesus that deep care is right here, where he walks, and that deep care engages deeply with what we are and where we are. This shows us the way forward: not to over-analyse what the Church should do, but to learn what next to do through direct engagement with him who meets us where we are. This takes patience and waiting.

It is not that we should curtail our theological work, but that to fulfil our theological task we must open it to direct engagement with him. This way, not only we, but also our theological constructions, encounter the limits of finite reasoning. Engaging Jesus, we are rationally puzzled and frustrated as well as healed. The puzzlement should not discourage our reasoning but re-direct our attention to patterns of order in the world we may not previously have noticed: the patterns of Jesus' walking. What patterns are these? And who moves this way? Asking these questions in the presence of Jesus is not only to consider what may be new subjects of theological inquiry, but also to practise what may be a new form of inquiry. We discover that to observe and examine the patterns of Jesus' walking is also, in some way, to live them. Our theological inquiry engenders relational abduction, which means that, if it is to continue further, it will lose its commitment to detachment, which now appears increasingly as having been a commitment to reason's self-attraction, which is resistance to divine attraction. From this moment on, if the inquiry is to continue further, it will name itself not only 'inquiry', but also 'being healed'. If it continues further, it may also come to name itself 'healing' and seek others who may seek healing; and this inquiry may appear to others as a kind of walking, wandering from person to person.

There are signs that enable an inquirer to recognize when theological inquiry may possibly be taken up into this kind of healing-walking.[6] One sign is that others may observe and comment on the inquirer's outer patterns of walking-healing. Another sign is that the inquirer may discover an inner sense of integrity and joy. A third sign is that the inquirer may begin to see light in the people he or she encounters. The night before I dictated these words,[7] I enjoyed a particularly wonderful time with this light: a steady awareness of inner peace, joy and outer light.

The wandering ecclesia: measured by Jesus' steps

The pilgrim who finds him- or herself walking-healing is not walking alone but together with the Church. If, as I suggested earlier, eucharistic worship embodies the inner measure of the Church as pilgrim, we may now speak of walking-healing with Jesus as the inner measure of the individual as pilgrim. The two measures are of course one: the individual pilgrim shares in the Church's eucharistic communion and (as noted in Chapter 3) eucharistic communion extends beyond the sanctuary into all the daily actions of its members. If this implies that the individual pilgrim is measured by the Eucharist, it implies that the Church too is measured by Jesus' walking-healing. The Church should itself imitate Jesus by walking around, embodying a presence on that actual land.

To imitate Jesus' walking-healing, the Anglican Church *cannot* be land-bound, sitting, for example, only in the British Isles. It must wander the land freely, and that includes the land of Israel–Palestine. The Anglican Vicar of Baghdad, the Revd Canon Andrew White, was a good model of this, offering his broad witness *in situ*, bearing witness to Jesus' caring in his wandering on the ground. The Anglican Church must become a wandering ecclesia. Such an ecclesia has inner and outer order but on the move, a mobile order. Its order is measured and guided by Scripture, by the Eucharist and by Jesus' steps. The Church's walking is not haphazard; it is *careful walking*, for it is walking by the Spirit, displaying Jesus' care to whoever follows, and also walking by the guidance of Scripture and the Eucharist. Just as the Anglican Church has a sense of responsibility for everybody in the land of the United Kingdom, so too the Church universal has responsibility for everybody in the land of Israel–Palestine, and that includes the Anglican communion within the Church universal. In this regard, the Anglican Church has shown some lethargy as well as some concern to 'keep its hands clean'. But it must not worry about such things; it is a moving Church and must move to engage with the people of the Holy Land, one to one.

Such walking does not preclude theological reflection: theologians of a walking Church wander first and then think theologically and practically in response to what they have found. Whoever or whatever turns up as they walk, whatever they find as they go along, these become the found realities in response to which they think and act. This is comparable to the order of reading Scripture and sharing in the Eucharist: theological reflection comes only after the theologian shares in God's word. There is also one further intermediary between the finding and the reflecting: this is imagining. To move off one's chair is first to be able to imagine walking.

Before it moves from its tendency to sit in place, the Church must first be prepared to imagine what it would be like to engage with others in the land, rather than shying away. The first goal is to stimulate and awaken the ecclesial imagination. To ask how this awakening begins is to return to our defining question: how is a person or a church able to turn away from self-attraction back to its primordial attractions to God and to others? My Coleridgian reply was that the first step is 'rational frustration, a sense that we are not doing what we ought to do' which leads us to search within our experience for signs of new patterns of order and unity. For the Anglican Church to become a walking Church, one first step would be an unfettered look at conditions today in the Holy Land. Observing the conditions of strife between Palestinians and Israelis should be enough to stimulate rational frustration in the Church. That frustration should be enough to stimulate the Church to search *in that land and among its peoples* (rather than merely in its memory) for signs of some new patterns of order and unity; and that searching should be enough to stimulate the Church to reshape its imagination by receiving new images of what this order and unity might be. Re-reading the Gospel narrative of Jesus' walking should be enough to re-introduce the Church to what appear to be the appropriate images: Jesus' walking-healing in the Holy Land. Examining those images closely, the Church may find that the examining is ineluctably embodied in the doing: that in this new seeing the Church finds itself already moving off its chair and walking toward the Holy Land.[8]

For a first glimpse of what this walking might be like, members of the Church may want to observe a practice called 'Scriptural Reasoning' (SR)[9] which takes place on the soil of the United Kingdom! Members of the Society for Scriptural Reasoning™ gather in small groups of Muslims, Christians and Jews to study together excerpts from all three Abrahamic scriptures. Introduced to the UK over a decade ago by the Cambridge Inter-faith Programme, SR is now practised by approximately eight groups or societies in the UK and approximately 20 more in North America and some other parts of the world. Groups consistently report that the practice tends simultaneously to increase the depth of each member's sense of intimacy with his or her own scriptural tradition at the same time that it opens each member's appreciation for the other scriptures and love for the other members. For Anglican participants, this practice may very well represent a first step in the Church's walking into the Holy Land to meet its peoples one to one in imitation of Jesus. A next step may be to walk within the Land itself, to practise whatever mode of engagement and witness is stimulated by the presence of another alongside, and then another.

A moving ecclesiology

To conduct a moving ecclesiology – to think 'the wandering Church' – is to theologize only in concrete relation to what the Church has been and may be. This is to offer a theology of sociopoiesis that is linked to possibility – the capacity of the divine to transform all of humanity – but which is concretized with respect to the actual life of the Church in history and right now, and moves forward eschatologically. For the Anglican Church to enact a moving ecclesiology is for it to allow its worldly architecture (both literally and figuratively) to be shaped and reshaped in response to where it finds itself and what it finds there. The architecture of the Church has seized up, its growth obstructed by too many decades of self-attraction; it is time for the Church, in spirit and body, to re-find its primordial attraction to God and to the other. When it does so, I imagine that its architecture will achieve new mobile forms, even like Ezekiel's chariot, or the waters that flow from underneath Jerusalem.

I have tried for many years to draw diagrams of how socio-poiesis works, when it moves forward in time, stretched forward by the Spirit. I have sensed that written ecclesiologies tended to look too much like snapshots – rather static and turgid images of the Church as seen from only one perspective and in only one moment of time. Following Coleridge, I sensed that, ironically, visual diagrams are less frozen because they claim to depict nothing more than images whose concrete meanings are displayed only when they are applied to making concrete judgements about the actual life of the Church as it finds itself in each moment of time. Such judgements also test the strength of the images and suggest ways that the diagrams may need to be redrawn to remain faithful, at once, to Scripture and to lived experience. The most comprehensive diagram I have drawn of sociopoiesis appears in Chapter 2, Figure 1.[10] There, the temporal movement of socio-poiesis is marked by 'arrows of attraction that draw each element of civilization to God and that animate the various dimensions of God's relation to us . . . each arrow points from the creator toward the creature and from one dimension of creaturely and civilizational life to another'.

Figure 2, 'The Lord and the World',[11] depicts the archetype of all temporal movement: from divine intensity to divine extensity, which is, at once, the movement of attraction from extensity to intensity.

Moving from Scripture and ecclesial history, to diagrams, to the lived experience of the Church, the ecclesiologist may be moved to formulate working guidelines for how to maintain a moving ecclesiology. I will offer here a few illustrations of what such guidelines may look like:

• A moving ecclesia must be reparative, which means that it must promote healing at a very deep level.

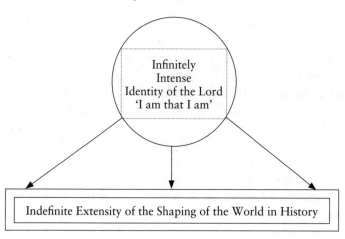

Figure 2 The Lord and the World[11]

- A theology of the moving Church is a theology set in motion by observations of the living Church; it moves the theologian's imagination and judgement; and its movement contributes directly to movement in the Church. In sum, the Church moves, the theology moves, church movement becomes new theology and the theology's movement contributes to the new Church.

- A moving ecclesiology of the Anglican Church should seek to avoid the potential obstructions to movement that have arisen in the history of each of the empirical churches. In recent times, for example, the Anglican Church has been challenged by a tendency to immobility, substituting far-reaching statements for far-reaching movement. The Roman Catholic Church is challenged now by a tendency to move only according to uniform doctrine. In this way, it is still too beholden to Aristotelian models of knowledge and too reluctant to adopt post-Newtonian as well as post-Aristotelian models that more accurately reflect the dynamism inherent in our knowledge not only of the created world but also of the divine word. The 'Oxford church' of Radical Orthodoxy tends to display a mixture of competing attractions: both these Aristotelian tendencies and those we are recommending for a moving ecclesia. With its great emphasis on *semper reformanda*, the United Reformed Church displays significant features of a moving ecclesia, always in a process of reformation. But this Church is also challenged today by a tendency to understand movement too literally, as if ecclesia, eucharistic sacrament and architecture itself were features only of the static Church and could not share in and help guide the moving Church. An imbalanced fear of non-movement can also engender self-attraction.

• A moving ecclesia must move its members to engage others within the Church and without, forming new relations and offering care and witness in the manner of Jesus' walking. The project of Receptive Ecumenism – conceived in the past few years by Paul Murray and sponsored by Durham University and the Roman Catholic Diocese of Hexham and Newcastle there together with many other institutions – illustrates such movement within the Church universal. In a paper prepared for the inaugural conference on Receptive Ecumenism, I wrote:

> Our ecumenical situation today is traceable to what has happened over the past millennium both within and outside church life: for complex religious and social reasons, not only theological differences, the *one Church* has become *many*, a Church related even in multiplicity has been replaced by *disconnected ecclesial units*, and the churches have been displaced from the public domain, especially in modern times. When measured by the expectations applicable to those who in Christ look forward to the kingdom of God, furthermore, the relations between these units, as well as their efficacy separately and collectively in the world at large, have usually been much less than might be expected to be the case: often the rationales offered for the churches have disallowed mutual understanding and respect except where imposed by other parties (a state, for example) or – more important – have failed to bring *structured co-presence, mutual support and mutual compassion*, and even *love*, between them; and these publicly discredit the churches and diminish their mission in the world . . .

Receptive Ecumenism promises to be a welcome move in addressing such issues as they now affect the Church: 'what it means for the Church – both the Church collectively and for Christians personally – to be called to discern together the living truth of "God's ways with the world" in a postmodern situation.'[12] It is distinctive in two ways at least: It opens the Roman Catholic Church to what may be learned through encounter with other Christian traditions, which denotes a readiness to *place* that Church *amongst* the churches, in a fashion parallel to Vatican II's renewal of the engagement of the Church with history. It also engages with the ecclesiological and theological questions which arise *for and from* the Church as it confronts secular counterparts and postmodern critique.[13]

My essay on Receptive Ecumenism was also the occasion for sketching the diagram of sociopoiesis reproduced above in Chapter 2. As I noted earlier, the complex levels of the diagram are meant to reflect the dynamism of a moving ecclesiology, just the kind of ecclesiology that is embodied in the Receptive Ecumenism project.

The project of Scriptural Reasoning illustrates how members of the Church may engage deeply with members of the other Abrahamic traditions. Such engagement must itself remain dynamic, since an Abrahamic gathering is no less liable to self-attraction than any gathering of the Church. Academic participants in SR must therefore, for example, extend their conversations to include the laity very broadly, as well as including religious and socio-political leaders of the communities. All need to be opened to the attractive light of God. The same may be said of the individual churches and of the broader Church bodies: all need to promote dialogue of the deepest sort between Church society and civil society.

One of the most recent forms of inter-religious engagement is Muslim–Christian dialogue, as illustrated by the recent statement, *A Common Word Between Us and You* and by the ongoing project of conversation that it has stimulated.[14] Extending many of the practices of SR, *A Common Word* illustrates additional ways in which the study of Scripture may help Christians – and Muslims – turn from paths of religious self-attraction to find God again as other and through love of the other. Like the other forms of engagement, this practice, too, is liable to its own self-attraction. My reflections on this form of inter-religious engagement therefore provide another occasion for suggesting how a moving ecclesiology – or sociopoiesis – may keep moving.

- *A Common Word* invites Christians to join Muslims in cele-brating the two communities' parallel loves of God and of neighbour. It invites members of the two communities to share these loves, in part, through the study of Scripture. Our read-ing of Matthew 9 would endorse this sharing as expressing what it may be to imitate Jesus' walking-healing. This imitation would apply to both parties in this shared study, since we do not read Matthew's Jesus as designating only what 'Christians' would do. In the setting of this shared study, Jesus designates the hospitality each party would extend to the other, and he designates the deepening of divine attraction and of healing that would be opened among them. In the midst of such study, something actually moves among the participants, and in its moving it attracts them and draws them into deeper witness and healing.

The participants' deeper witness to each other awakens them, as well, to the divisions that stand between them and the wounds that remain open. The shared study frees them to describe these wounds and attend to these divisions: not to move beyond them but to move into them in the face of Scripture. The words of Scripture may appear at times to reflect or promote rather than heal these divisions. The ensu-ing dialogue may be volatile and may awaken even more pain. Members of a single fellowship of study must therefore share sufficient time together that, in the face of Scripture and graced by what moves in their midst, their study and dialogue may at times open sources of knowledge and healing that lay even under these divisions and wounds. Drawing an analogy from medicine, I referred above and in the previous chapter to the process of 'granulation', in which the body generates new connective tissue from deep within the flesh, just underneath the diseased tissue that lies above it. On this occasion the analogy is to sources of healing that we pray may emerge beneath these wounds, from deep within the scriptural reading and within the biographies, socio-politics, hearts and spirits of these scriptural readers.

What will emerge between the gospel and the Qur'an remains to be seen: our ecclesiology rests on the anticipation and hope that painful dialogue may stimulate rational frustration in the face of the scriptural texts, that this frustration may stimulate ever more intense inquiry, that the inquirers will be drawn to observe new and unexpected patterns of order and unity, and that these patterns will attract them to the light that opens meanings and heals. The depth of rational frustration raised by such a study may most likely correspond to the depth of frustration raised by what the participants observe in their theopolitical contexts. Inquiry that responds to the first frustration may therefore offer resources for responding to the second. One resource would be the friendship and love that may arise among the participants. Another would be the depth of scriptural reading and comprehension that this friendship and love may encourage and support. Another would be the vibrancy of the divine word that may be made visible through this comprehension: an opening to the energy of the life of God, which flows among the participants and between the participants and the two scriptures. This energy is the source of all movement. When it emerges in such a dialogue, then it is a moving dialogue. We may observe the dialogue become walking, for true dialogue is always walking, the participants fellow-walkers.

Notes

1 The Reverend Suheil Dawani, whose diocese includes Israel, the Palestinian territories, Jordan, Syria and Lebanon, and whom I had met previously during his sabbatical in Cambridge.

2 Cf. Chapter 1, note 3.

3 Dr Mouneer Hanna Anis, who is also the new Bishop of Egypt (including North Africa and the Horn of Africa).

4 Chapter 3, pp. 69–70.

5 FC is most representative.

6 Note that for Coleridge 'abduction' refers to moments of reason's being 'taken up' (abducted) by the divine in this way. For inquiry to be taken up into healing-walking is for it to enter into relational abduction. See Chapter 3, p. 70; Chapter 4, pp. 82–5.

7 16 October 2007.

8 This is another way to understand divine abduction: these Gospel images abduct (carry away and draw into God) the Church's imagination and, with it, its tendencies to act.

9 See Chapter 1, note 12 for more details. For introductions to the practice of SR, see, inter alia, http://www.interfaith.cam.ac.uk//index.php (SR in the Cambridge Inter-faith Programme); http://etext.virginia.edu/journals/ssr/ (The Journal of Scriptural Reasoning); http://www.scripturalreasoning.org/ (Scriptural Reasoning in the UK); http://etext.lib.virginia.edu/journals/jsrforum/ (Scriptural Reasoning in North America).

10 Figure 1: The Energetics of Attraction (p. 48).

11 From 'Receptive Ecumenism: Learning by Engagement', in Paul D. Murray, ed., *Receptive Ecumenism and the Call to Catholic Learning: Exploring a Way for Contemporary Ecumenism*, Oxford: Oxford University Press, 2008, p. 433.

12 Paul D. Murray, 'On Valuing Truth in Practice: Rome's Postmodern Challenge', *International Journal for Systematic Theology* 8 (2006), pp. 163–83 (164); also in Laurence Paul Hemming and Susan Frank Parsons, eds, *Redeeming Truth: Considering Faith and Reason*, Aldershot: Ashgate, 2007. For an introduction to the Receptive Ecumenism project see http://www.centreforcatholicstudies.co.uk/?cat=6 (Durham University's Centre for Catholic Studies).

13 Hardy, 'Receptive Ecumenism', pp. 428–41.

14 For an introduction to *A Common Word*, see the official website of *A Common Word*, http://www.acommonword.com/. Hardy was deeply engaged in conversations about *A Common Word*, in particular with Aref Nayed (contributor to the original statement of *A Common Word*) and David Ford. See David Ford's response to *A Common Word* and to Muslim–Christian dialogue more broadly: 'Seeking Muslim, Christian and Jewish Wisdom in the Fifteenth, Twenty-first and Fifty-eighth Centuries: A Muscat Manifesto', delivered at The Sultan Qaboos Grand Mosque, Muscat, Oman, 20 April 2009: http://www.acommonword.com/OmanFordMuscatManifestocircverapro9.pdf. See also Aref Ali Nayed's response to Ford's 'Manifesto': 'Growing Ecologies of Peace, Compassion and Blessing: A Muslim Response', delivered at Cambridge University in 2009 and published online by the Cambridge Inter-faith Programme: http://www.interfaith.cam.ac.uk/en/resources/papers/ecologies-muslim-response-to-muscat-manifesto.

5

A Light in the Tunnel under Jerusalem:
A Eucharistic Pneumatology

Narrative: The Tunnel under the Temple Mount

Later in our visit to Jerusalem, we took a tour through the tunnel
that goes under the Temple Mount and down underneath it.
Through an entryway, we entered a tunnel that passes underneath and inside the Western Wall. The opening of the tunnel had
an introductory section, in which stood a model of the Temple
Mount. The tour guides introduced us to the model and then
led us along through a remarkable series of tunnels. It is hard to
imagine what we saw, because the tunnels were halfway inside
the walls. One became aware of the height of the wall, of the
stages in its construction, and of the huge antiquity of the lower
part. The experience is all somewhat indefinite: a presentation of
long periods of history, whose antiquity emerges stage by stage
through the tunnels' descent.

Our guides introduced us to this history by reading or para-
phrasing the literature provided for such tours. They spoke of

the Temple Mount as the focal point of creation, the place where Adam came into being and where Abraham served God. Jerusalem was chosen by God as the dwelling place of the *shekhinah*, 'the indwelling presence of the Lord'; David acquired Jerusalem and the mount; Solomon built the Temple on it, which housed the ark of the covenant; it was razed by the Babylonians and rebuilt seventy years later as the Second Temple; that Temple was razed by the Romans in AD 70, after which the Western Wall remained as its only remnant. Jews prayed in the shadow of the Western Wall, expressing their faith that the Temple would be rebuilt here and that the divine presence remained here. The Wall has become a focus of prayer for Jews all over the world. A plaque is affixed to the entrance of the tunnel, bearing the text of Psalm 122:

> I rejoiced with those who said to me,
>   'Let us go to the house of the LORD.'
> Our feet are standing
>   in your gates, O Jerusalem.
> Jerusalem is built like a city
>   that is closely compacted together.
> That is where the tribes go up,
>   the tribes of the LORD,
>   to praise the name of the LORD
>   according to the statute given to Israel.
> There the thrones for judgment stand,
>   the thrones of the house of David.
> Pray for the peace of Jerusalem:
>   'May those who love you be secure.
> May there be peace within your walls
>   and security within your citadels.'
> For the sake of my brothers and friends,
>   I will say, 'Peace be within you.'
> For the sake of the house of the LORD our God,
>   I will seek your prosperity.[1]

The tunnel initiated a project beyond mere archaeology and sociology. It stripped away centuries, revealing the entire length of the Western Wall in all its glory (448 metres long, with one stone reaching a length of 60 metres), many rooms, a section of the Second Temple road, a pool and many other finds. All of this should one day serve as a meeting centre for learning. I knew beforehand of the huge, polished and smoothly fitted-together brace of stones, which made the Temple what it was. But I did not anticipate the impact of experiencing them in this setting. It was enormously impressive. From the very beginning of the tunnel, it is evident how very carefully the construction was done. The high centre of the ceiling is arched, and the walls on each side are beautifully finished. This was not slam–bang construction. It was very carefully wrought, over a long time frame, the way cathedrals were crafted, and this was thousands of years before. It was all so carefully measured: a place of extraordinary history.

As I gazed on the walls, I began to see unpredictable lights on each side, especially along the right side where the stones are large, perhaps two metres square, and well finished, with variable colours, predominantly beige-brown or yellowish with whiteness that shows in the light. This is Jerusalem stone, the kind that changes hue according to how it is cut and how the light is refracted. Traditionally, the stone was held to display a living quality because of its refractive capacity and responsiveness to changes in light. Each part of each stone therefore shows its particularity in time and space; one experiences light moving over it, drawing one's attention to its individuality.

I was most interested in the way God's presence appeared through this span of time in the Temple architecture and in the very stones that measured it. It was like a long strand of history irradiated by what one imagined to be the divine presence. This meant that the whole experience was consistently bright for me with the light of God. Within the stones was embedded the intensity of the light of God. My experience was shaped in part by what I learned from our guide and the accompanying literature about the huge significance of Jerusalem. For me, it was a narrative of Jerusalem's special significance as measured by God for his purposes. This was my gloss over the whole thing, reintegrating my reflections in Jericho on the special significance of the land as measured by God. These thoughts were still on my mind and became even more central in my time in Jerusalem. The site was not simply of historical interest. The place invoked God's purposes more firmly than I had ever perceived before.

As for the experience of light itself, I had known previously about Mircea Eliade's phenomenological approach to religious experience.[2] But there is a sharp difference between his approach and what I experienced, which was not merely phenomenological, but true in a much deeper sense. I experienced something that moved beyond what appears phenomenally to a place of more direct truth. In my awareness, the tunnels under the Temple were incomparably more than just archaeological artefacts; they displayed a deeper level of truth as it actually entered history. This reflection was new to me and was allied with a strange sense of the intensity of light there. The tunnels were artificially lit in a particular way, but what I saw was not just the light that the installation provided. There was something more embedded within the rock. It is tricky to speak of 'light embedded'. Is this an external sensation or something else? I don't know. The experience could be taken as something mystical, in the sense of something less than reality; or it can concern reality itself.

To some extent I was attracted to the shape of the rock. Already lagging behind the group, I had limited time to focus on it; so I moved along more quickly. I was reluctant to be swept on so fast. I preferred to linger, but the intensity of the experience increased with my movement. The rock seemed to be expressing its own intensity. But the more intense it became, the more I would be forced to use another language to refer to it than language about rock and stone. At this point, my experience was less and less of the rock and more of something of increasingly wide importance. It was of light and of the purposes of God.

Once again, I cannot employ phenomenological language to clarify my experience, since that language seems to intrude on the reality of what I saw. Phenomenology is a particular, philosophically based consideration that belongs to itself rather than to the material it examines. This material requires a more direct form of observation and appreciation, less humanly constrained and subjective. This is not to say that an account of light would be non-theoretical. I do not yet know what theoretical discourse would be most helpful, but I assume it would address issues of energy.

What is this that shines through all things? The most useful vocabulary for answering this question appears to belong to physics: not physics only in the strict sense as natural science and *techne*, but physics also as a source of tropes to be applied to the experience. Defined strictly as a discrete science, the *techne* of physics – like phenomenology – serves itself more than the material of this experience. I find the language of physics useful when applied to more general use, as I have applied tropes from physics, systems theory, quantum mechanics and evolutionary theory in a number of writings, for example *God's Ways with the World*.

I am interested in the public uses of scientific theory, which I believe speak more directly to experiences like this than the strictly specialized practices of scientific analysis. I mean uses that speak to what tends to be our common experience, which is what both Coleridge and Charles Peirce identify as the appropriate subject matter of philosophy.[3] To use scientific languages in this way is to refine our metaphysics in a holistic way, clarifying our elemental assumptions about the shape of our world and our existence. Classical metaphysics does this when it talks about relations: a category that applies to classical physics but also to Trinitarian theology, to human engagements and to performative discourse – relational terms used to effect action and draw people closer together. This is the way metaphysical vocabulary works in Coleridge and Peirce's philosophy and the way I would employ it: articulating general wonderments that also have practical force, expressing the full sphere of human experience, knowing and doing, and integrating all these into the ultimate sources. Coleridge employs diagrams in this comprehensive way: to trace human experience from the most rudimentary to the most developed, including trajectories of cognition and of affections, in service to the personal integrity of a thinker drawn to the attractive force of the divine.[4] This is my goal as well: to offer unrestricted descriptions that do not reduce the scope of experience but help open restricted languages to the integrity and fullness of both cognition and the affections.

To articulate my experience of light I therefore want to employ theoretical vocabularies that will help identify what it is that shines through all existence. In this effort I come to appreciate the enormous intensity of the divine. To describe how that intensity attracts us, I adopt the language of physical light and its energy. Because we all experience this inordinate energy, this language enables us to speak intelligibly about the fullness of the divine and the fullness of the divine purpose as it is evident in some tangible thing. One can speak of divine purpose in terms of both its own superabundant energy and how this energy actually shapes the way things are. I am inclined to talk about this shaping in the language of 'attraction', of the way the very intensity of God's light attracts creation to be itself, enabling each thing (technically each 'relative density') to be itself. This means that existence is intrinsically differentiated, so that each thing is attracted to be itself at the same time that each and all are attracted to God. If one speaks of God's creating all things, then in this sense each *thing* – rather than any composite of things – is the subject of what we call divine attraction. A grain of sand is a thing that can be attracted to God, while a bunch of sand is a composite, not itself the subject of attraction. In these terms, a person is also a created thing, attracted in its integrity to its creator. To be attracted to God is to have one's person-ness intensified as one is, in one's created individuality. To be attracted is to be more what one ultimately is, and I call this entering into one's own *vocation*. In my vocabulary, 'vocation' is an ultimate term for that in which a person is most fully attracted to God.

Narrative: More on the Gradual Emergence of Light

It happened at first without anybody interpreting it as such and it never was interpreted, except by me. It was a manifestation that began to assume its own importance, so that it was in a sense self-presenting, self-interpreting – and more intensively so as time went on, denser and more focused. Some of this experience may have happened during the night-time, when it bore itself in on me, because it was somehow embedded in me. But something had imprinted itself on me during the day. In one sense, these were ordinary days, visiting like a tourist, going here and there and seeing things. But, in another sense, something was happening through the everyday, which was not only the seeing of ordinary things. It was almost palpable at times. I felt I could reach up and gather the light that appeared to me. And then I could adopt the light as a subject of prayer: to pray, for example, for people to be gathered into that light.

During the night, I was conscious, in a kind of half-sleep, of an experience of almost a shaft of light: sometimes discrete and focused, sometimes 'broadband', so that everything was illuminated. I would wake up and the experience would continue. This was unusual, because I am not a dreaming sort of person (unlike Deborah, who has vivid dreams, which she can interpret; I do not). These were not dreams, but impressions that awakened me and continued outside of sleep. Gradually, I became aware of these impressions during the day. It is difficult to chart the growth of this experience, but I recall that it became very vivid: not just light, but light within the things around me and emerging from them. In this way, Jerusalem became a shining city for me, increasingly irradiated with light, of both a general and specific character, suffused and infused.

I have for years experienced light suffused around other people, especially in a pastoral context. The light I experienced in Jerusalem was of this kind – emanating from entities outside me – except that now it was the stones of the city and not only persons and now the intensity was enormous. This experience remains significant for me pastorally as a light to be observed in or around others, and the greater intensity suggests to me the possibility of greater opportunities to search with others about their concerns and vocations. At the same time, now I also experience the light separated from others, in itself and then suffusing and illuminating virtually everything. I believe this frees my pastoral activity, extending something I have observed in the last year or two: that I am freer to work with people more broadly on issues of vocation. This includes graduate students, with whom I find that our pastoral discussions move further away from academic topics and allow students to make vocational discoveries of their own. I say this is 'freer', because the light is less attached to the immediate and particular concerns of the people with whom I am speaking, displaying its own power and location as a resource that may open new possibilities for them in whatever they are doing. They may begin to discover the light in them, within which they are not predefined.

Theological Reflections: The Experience of Light as Divine Call

Imagine a person engaged in everyday life, for example walking along observing the stones on a wall in Jerusalem. After the fact, the person may recall that, gradually, a certain quality of the stones *drew his attention* and that quality of *attraction* steadily increased. In this case, the quality is something sensed (light *and* its attractiveness): the light attracts increasingly intense attention. Some time later, through another recollection, the attractiveness of the light appears as an independent subject of attention. Now the person attends to the light and its pure attractiveness rather than to the rock, so that, in subsequent experiences of the rock, the light and attractiveness appear as immediate subjects of attention. Then, through another recollection, and with memory of scriptural analogues, the light and its attractiveness may appear as a *call*: the call of God and of the Spirit. If so, a more radical transformation will have taken place: the person will no longer appear as the subject of this experience, but as if someone else, the one called into God's service. This is a taste of the relativity of identity in the engagement with God in the world. In the mode of 'being called', I would experience everything as illuminated, not just the rock. The world itself calls one to God's light.

Theological Reflections: Darkness and Our Failings Before the Light

After these encounters with light, what concerns me now is not who has it right or wrong – whose calling and whose religion is the true one – but that we have all failed, all the religions. The world is sinking. This reality strikes me hard and struck me very hard in Israel: that by failing to be attracted to the light we are slipping into darkness. This downward movement is not inevitable or necessary, but by now we have a long track record of moving

this way. My experience of light is accompanied by an awareness of how dark we are outside the light. In some ways, my time
in Israel was therefore very difficult. While there was that amazing experience of light, I was at the same time more powerfully
aware of wrongness than ever before: not localized but applied
to all humanity. The more powerfully I experienced the light,
the more powerfully I was moved by a sense of disappointment
and, more than that, of failure: a sense of the weightiness of the
whole world, which, having failed to live up to the light, was
being carried down into greater darkness. This darkness envelops
the churches, as well, which do not manifest signs of having being
drawn to the light. Instead, they have sought to understand the
world's ills in strictly naturalist ways, to repair things by seeking
to understand the causes of everything rather than opening themselves to divine attraction.

Living up to the light does not mean living as an angel. Being
attracted is a creaturely thing, wholly on our level. As I indicate in
the diagram of sociopoiesis (Figure 1 in Chapter 2, p. 48), all the
worldly dimensions of theopolitical life (the entire lower half of
the diagram) are dimensions of worldly work in the light. In light
of this light, I see more clearly that our failure is simply not to
open ourselves to our primordial attractions as God's creatures.
Just being in the Church is not enough without this opening and
without thereby being found by the light. In the simplest terms,
this means we are called within the Church to take worship more
seriously, to take the text of Scripture more seriously, and to be
found by what is happening in Scripture. It is not a matter of
which ecclesial institutions we build or enact but how fully these
institutions operate in relation to the light. Each entity and relation I identify in the diagram must be opened to the light: opened,
as we saw previously, to temporal abduction and to the terrific
upward movements that would be made possible by this abduction. The Church and its theologians, as well as the supervening
governments, fail do their task in this way; they are, moreover,
befuddled about how to do any better. So – aware that something
is wrong and not knowing what to do – they relapse into competition: each church championing its way, as if arguing more for
its own way would somehow resolve its problems, rather than

rediscovering how to open its way to the divine light. As far as Anglicanism is concerned, the Church wishes for simple solutions to problems that do not yield simple solutions.[5] What do we have instead? We have people in the States and worldwide who want simple, either/or fixes, issuing statements, documents and arguments: all of these more expressions of extensity, further obstructing the Church rather than opening it to its primordial attractions.

It was the sum total of all this that gave me a sense of the huge power of God's light and energy and how the divine is at work. But the question is, 'How to get it across?!' This power is an infinitely probing, penetrating thing. What is it that attracts someone to something 'better?' I have a strong sense that goodness simply draws them to something fuller; it is an opening and enabling process, a recognition of and attraction to life and to the source of life within. It is like a granulation of patterns, words, light, senses: things 'percolating up' just like the waters of the Jordan, and there is a whole range of things coming to the surface, with a new awareness of the simple wonder and beauty of creation and life itself and, with that, the awareness of how little we have 'got it right'. With the light comes sadness and loss but also a yearning to live from this source and to be oriented to it: to the life and health bubbling up deep within. The sense of sorrow is sharing in the grief of God and his longing for the best for his people and the world: a longing for us not to be distracted or to waste time. It is about recognizing how much more there is than we have ever seen before and about being attracted by it and lifted up to it. This light is something that is capable of lifting one deeply from within: that is what I mean by 'attraction'.

A striking feature of the light is its inherent openness and its being non-exclusive. We cannot contain the light, however much we might want to or try to. Remember YHWH, 'I am who I am and I shall be who I shall be.' Our human attempts to hold and define God become inimical to the light. We cannot grasp hold. It is like trying to grasp Israel for the Jews. It is one thing to have a homeland, but quite another to possess it and restrict it. Think what it is like to have a child: it is a gifting of responsibility.

So, what is it to indwell somewhere and have a homeland without possessing it? How can we participate honestly in the huge reality of the light without needing to possess it? The divine light lifts you to something you do not need to possess, lifting you to another sphere. It enters you non-possessively and filters up within you. We are regenerated: transformed and rebuilt from deep within.

People do not believe that things can be renewed in this way. They are too stuck, too fixed: the heavy imprint of materialism that most people live with. But what if we were freed from that? What if we were given new categories and could shift away from the Aristotelian 'fixed units of measure' to something new altogether?⁶ People are often habitually drawn away from the light. How, therefore, with all the leaves falling, covering up and 'burying' the light, how do we uncover it? This is our tragedy: extensity. We are caught up in one thing after another and then another. When we meet someone who is open and drawn into this light, whose eyes are opened to 'see', it is not just about his/her personal experience: something is happening in that person on behalf of humanity, and he/she is making an authentic contribution that is to be shared, not held privately. To receive a good and not share it is to lessen it. To receive this light is thus to share it; it is about sharing and participating in the depths of God and God's goodness, indefinitely and infinitely. That is where things get really exciting: there is a depth in God that is fathomless; that is where it gets quite dazzling. What might be! The infinite potential of the world. We limit ourselves so much! But the invitation is to get caught up in the re-creative Spirit of the Trinity.

The world has huge potential that it has sunk away from. Nonetheless, it is important not to focus on the remedial, but rather on the huge potential: God's goodness and Spirit at work in and among us! We need to be clever in the ways of the world and to see what has gone wrong and even perhaps why. But we also need not to get stuck there. It is a matter of identifying the blockages and then moving on. It is easy to get stuck in the blockages rather than focusing on the wonder and glory and vision of God and getting swept up and caught up in it. It is not a matter of our working out every detail of how to move on; we need to leave room for the Spirit to work.

There is a strong temporal thrust of movement forward: a 'perfecting movement'[7] toward the fullness of God's creation and God's work, far beyond what we can see. What is the fullness of God's work with the world? That is plainly what it is all directed to. There is a large panoply of things that need to be attended to.[8] The dynamic is there, but we have to participate in it and identify what is involved in it. It is partly a matter of being swept up in and by it, but it is also a matter of acknowledging that these responsibilities are there. So often we get distracted. What is it that both attracts and limits the Church? It has become over-concentrated on its 'inner meaning'. We need to learn how to persist with our task in the world. What are the essentials of this? Opening up the true potential and resources of human life. Liturgy is one way of facilitating and helping people enter into this creative dynamic and drawing them deeper into the light, letting it penetrate and irradiate them. But this opening is certainly not exclusive to the Church: there are lots of other ways, too, and we need to recognize and interpret them in public life. It is about how the Church relates to the world.

Coda

1 When, with my current illness, I became the one my family cared for at home, it was as if the extended family became a congregation at home, gathered around its pastor. This time, however, the pastor needed their care and healing. The result of this taught me a great deal about pastoral healing. The family's work was to do physical things for me, like moving furniture, moving the bed, placing me in this room or that. The lesson may be that, when a pastor presents himself as pastor, offering care to members of the community, they, in their receptivity and in that sense passivity, remain individuals. But when the pastor is himself in need of physical care and the members of the community bustle about providing it collectively, then they in their activity become members of a community; they become a church. It is as if they become a church when they are measured by the common purpose of providing physical care; in that sense, their helping a family member was like building a temple. When I am represented by my

voice and word, I remain pastor to members of my family; they are passive and need healing. But when I am represented by my body and have earthly needs – the one for whom they move a bed or chair – then *they* become active and, in their common activity, they become a church. There is here a lesson in how suffering may be transformed into healing. When Jesus suffers in the flesh and becomes a place of need, then those he cared for are transformed, from individuals with needs into active members of the Church. By caring for Jesus and imitating Jesus in his care for others, those he cared for become active care-givers and active members of the caring Church.

2 Within a church in crisis, congregation members may, in this way, be transformed from being individuals who have needs and are cared for by the pastor to being individuals whom he cannot fully care for, since their problems concern their relations with one another, and the pastor is not a miracle worker: his pastoral care is not the kind that introduces new conditions of sociopoiesis. For the church to begin to heal, the pastor must be transformed, from one who actively pastors individuals to one who serves as representative of the congregation's woundedness and who opens himself to becoming an agent of whatever transforming and healing spirit makes itself known within the life of the church. Only then might individual congregants be prepared to turn from attending to their own needs and losses to tending the needs of the congregation, from being passive recipients of care to becoming potentially active agents of the Spirit. This is a type of the turning which we characterized earlier, from self-attraction to divine attraction and thus attraction to others. It is no simple or immediate or predictable thing. It is not a matter of mere choice, or will, or rational discipline. It is perhaps the central drama in our ecclesiology: when a pilgrim's openness to the Spirit is met by the Spirit and 'other' replaces 'self' as the object of attraction. This is still not the end of the drama – no step in it is the mechanical consequence of a previous one – but only the beginning of the possibility of healing: an opening for attraction to meet attraction and, with the balm of the Spirit, for a wounded Church to walk with Jesus.

Notes

1 Scripture taken from the *Holy Bible, New International Version* ®. Copyright © 1973, 1978, 1984 Biblica. Used by permission of Zondervan. All rights reserved.

2 For a look at Eliade's phenomenological approach to religion, see, for example, Mircea Eliade, with Willard R. Trask and Jonathan Z. Smith, *The Myth of The Eternal Return: Cosmos and History*, Princeton: Princeton University Press, 2005; Mircea Eliade, with Willard R. Trask, *The Sacred and The Profane: The Nature of Religion*, New York: Harcourt Brace Jovanovich, 1987.

3 While devoting most of his time to laboratory sciences and the logic of science, Peirce argued that the sciences are built on first premises derived from everyday life in society. He drew a sharp distinction between philosophy, which he dubbed *coenoscopy*, or the study of common experience, and the sciences, which he dubbed *idioscopy*, or 'special sciences', which prosecute and articulate their investigations through technical languages meaningful only to small communities of inquiry. Peirce argued that each mode of study had its own place. He was critical both of 'seminarians', who sought to make claims about the natural world without technical grounding in any of the special sciences of their day, and, especially, of the positivist thinkers who forgot that the sciences of nature draw their first premises from everyday social life and return to that life, in the end, as the source of final judgement on the usefulness and worth of science and its fruits. Peirce argued, moreover that the ultimate measure of these everyday judgements is the word of the creator God alone.

Coleridge anticipated Peirce in this dual attention to science and to the wholeness of life, except that he was more vigilant in noting the weight of the divine presence in each aspect of science and of everyday life. In a paper on Hardy's study of Coleridge's *Opus Maximum*, David Ford captures Hardy's love of Coleridge's devotion to the whole of things:

> I can easily believe, that there are more invisible than visible Beings in the universe. But who shall describe for us their families? and their ranks and relationships and distinguishing features and functions? What they do? where they live? The human mind has always circled around a knowledge of these things, never attaining it. I do not doubt, however, that it is sometimes beneficial to contemplate, in thought, as in a Picture, the image of a greater and better world; lest the intellect, habituated to the trivia of daily life, may contract itself too much, and wholly sink into trifles. But at the same time we must be vigilant for truth, and maintain proportion, that we may distinguish certain from uncertain, day from night.

The opening quotation is from the Epigraph to *The Rime of the Ancient Mariner* (1817) taken from Thomas Burnet's *Archaeologie Philosophicae* (1692) about 'the sum of existing things' (33). Hardy sees it summarizing the dilemma Coleridge faced in his work, trying to do justice to the scope of reality, which 'includes both the material and social worlds with the Divine, understood both in themselves and as interpenetrating in Reason and moral will'

(34). Yet people find this scope difficult to handle: '... questions of the sort Coleridge persisted in pursuing are simply set aside in the attempt to manage the complexities of life today ... Coleridge pursues them with such unremitting intensity of attention, thought and expression as to make them difficult for all but the most patient and careful.' As if that is not enough, 'there are still other and more fundamental challenges', such as Coleridge's insistence on always attending to the moral implications, and his conducting 'a continuous dialogue with current thought and practice in all domains, from the sciences of the day to the most profoundly religious'. One result is that 'even the most capable interpreters of Coleridge ... often subtly – even if unintentionally – underrate him' (34). (David Ford, 'Daniel Hardy and Scriptural Reasoning: Reflections on his Understanding of Coleridge's *Opus Maximum*', paper delivered for the Cambridge University Inter-faith Programme as part of the conference, 'The Fruitfulness of Dan Hardy's Thought for Scriptural Reasoning' (5–6 June 2008). Ford's citations are from Daniel W. Hardy, 'Harmony and Mutual Implication in the *Opus Maximum*' in Jeffrey W. Barbeau, ed., *Coleridge's Assertion of Religion: Essays on the* Opus Maximum, Leuven, Paris, Dudley, MA: Peeters, 2006, pp. 33–52.

4 See Chapter 2, note 2, pp. 54–5 for Hardy's comments on Coleridge's notions of attraction, abduction and diagramming.

5 Hardy adds, 'On the pressing issue of homosexuality in the Church, I admire Stacy Johnson, for example, for thinking to come up with non-simple solutions.' See Stacy Johnson, *A Time to Embrace: Same-Gender Relationships in Religion, Law, and Politics*, Grand Rapids, MI: Eerdmans, 2006.

6 Hardy argues that modern Western culture has been unduly influenced by the scientific world views of both Aristotle and Newton. He has in mind the influence, for example, of Aristotle's trust in uniform measure: namely, that measurement is based on the assumption and usefulness of some atomic units and that our understanding of such units is derived from number theory. For the general topic, see, for example, Aristotle's *Metaphysics* x.1–2; for applications to time see *Physics* iv.10–14. Hardy also has in mind the influence of Newton's assumption that movement can be measured by a standard unit (as discussed in Chapter 3, pp. 60–1, 65). On Newton's understanding of measure and its relation to inertia, see, for example, Isaac Newton, *The Principia: Mathematical Principles of Natural Philosophy*, Berkeley, CA: University of California Press, 1999; Robert Disalle, 'Newton's Philosophical Analysis of Space and Time', in I. Bernard Cohen and George E. Smith, eds, *The Cambridge Companion to Newton*, Cambridge: Cambridge University Press, 2002, pp. 41–3 (33–56); and Bernard Cohen, 'Newton's Concepts of Force and Mass', in *The Cambridge Companion*, pp. 58–71 (57–84). While recognizing the usefulness of standard measures, Hardy argues that too many everyday practitioners as well as thinkers in the modern West have forgotten that use is defined by the user or, at least, by the context of use. His interest in Coleridge and Peirce is therefore complemented by his interest in the relational and context-dependent character of quantum measurement in physics. We had several very long and happy discussions, for example, of David Ritz Finkelstein, *Quantum Relativity: A Synthesis of the Ideas of Einstein and Heisenberg*, Berlin, Heidelberg, New

York: Springer Verlag, 1996. Hardy did not mean to exaggerate the differences between Newton and later science. He therefore took interest in Finkelstein's argument that 'Newton seems to have been the first to undertake to reconcile the particulate theory of light with [various] . . . conspicuously wavelike behavior[s]' (p. 156). Hardy's concern was that Western society rendered itself 'Newtonian' in ways that even Newton himself did not.

7 The notion of praise as 'perfecting perfection' appears in David F. Ford and Daniel W. Hardy, *Living in Praise: Worshipping and Knowing God*, Grand Rapids: Baker Academic, 2005 (1984), pp. 8f.

8 See, for example, Hardy's engagement with Paul Murray's 'Receptive Ecumenism' project: 'Receptive Ecumenism: Learning By Engagement', in Paul D. Murray, ed., *Receptive Ecumenism and the Call to Catholic Learning: Exploring a Way for Contemporary Ecumenism*, Oxford: Oxford University Press, 2008, pp. 428–41. And for the implications for Muslim–Christian theological dialogue, see David Ford, 'Seeking Muslim, Christian and Jewish Wisdom in the Fifteenth, Twenty-first and Fifty-eighth Centuries: A Muscat Manifesto', delivered at The Sultan Qaboos Grand Mosque, Muscat, Oman, 20 April 2009: http://www.acommonword.com/OmanFordMuscatManifestocircverapro9. pdf.

PART THREE

6

Living Theology in the Face of Death

David F. Ford in conversation with
Daniel W. Hardy

A lot has gone on that has brought my theology a lot further: that's what I want to see rounded off somehow. There is something waiting to happen, and that is what I want to see. The exact form is yet to be seen but that it needs to break forth is pretty clear to me.[1]

The conversations with Dan Hardy during the last six months of his life were extraordinary for all of us who took part in them – and it is worth remembering that this book draws only on those that he had with the three authors of this book, not the many others he had with his wife, Perrin, his three other children, his friends, his graduate students and the priest who was with him during the last days. This chapter is based on the conversations with me. Its main purpose is to help make sense of what he dictated to Peter Ochs (Chapters 2–5 above) but, in addition, to give some idea of how his theology was being 'rounded off somehow' during this time. I had never experienced anything like these conversations, and doing even partial justice to them is remarkably difficult.

I will first attempt to indicate what was so distinctive about them, then reflect on their types of discourse, their main concepts and symbols, Dan's emerging theology of the Church (ecclesiology) and the character of the 'church' of collegial friendship, which was exemplified in the conversations themselves, and his Spirit-led approach to God and the future of theology.

An Intense Integration of Theology and Life

I think the best way to begin to say what was distinctive about the conversations is that while he was having them he was simultaneously living out their content, and that content was the culmination of a lifetime combining Christian living and theological thinking. For example, he spoke of Coleridge 'looking for a moral life, a full life, total humanity, total Church, and total God', and we studied together the volume of Coleridge's *Collected Works* with the 1828 diagram of the 'Schema of the Total Man'.[2] The themes of living morally with full integrity, and the fullness of life, of humanity, of the Church and of God, pervaded the conversations, and many aspects of those themes appear in this and other chapters. On all of them he was exploring new ideas, often with deep roots in his earlier theology; for example, his decades of studying and writing about Coleridge as a theological thinker led into his fresh thinking about abduction.

At the same time Dan was living something new in relation to each of them. During the final six months he energetically worked at family and academic responsibilities so as both to leave his affairs in good order and to have parting conversations. His sense of the fullness of life was infectious, ranging from nature (I remember sharing his delight during the last summer he had at his Twin Lakes house in Connecticut) through family meals (culminating in his last birthday celebration a few days before his death) to a passionate and critical concern for what was going on in the Cambridge Inter-Faith Programme. His own 'total humanity' was being shown in new ways, especially in a hitherto rare capacity to express feeling directly and physically, various other signs of the integration of mind and affections, his taking far more initiatives than usual in directing the flow of conversations, and a willingness to face some very painful memories and personal experiences.

A sustained theme during the six months was 'total Church'. He drew on the pilgrimage, multiple involvements with the church in Cambridge, the discussion with his daughter of her priesthood, his reconnection with General Theological Seminary, his continuing work with graduate students and the almost daily conversation with Peter Ochs. In conversation with me, one striking new ecclesial element was the way the other Abrahamic faiths were integrated with his ecclesiology; and, overall, his concept of 'fullness' and 'abundance', following Ephesians 1.23 and 3.20, challenged many ideas of the boundaries of the Church.

The integration of thought and life was evident in his enactment of such ideas even as he spoke about them: he was not only trying to define abduction (see below) but also exemplifying it in how he was exploring theological topics; likewise, he spoke about interpreting Scripture in the Spirit while doing it. He often expressed his sense of living within the abundance of God. Having spent many years in regular conversation with him about thanking and praising God, it was fascinating for me not just to revisit with him some of those themes but also to see the intensity and directness of his expressions of thanks and praise. The other side of this activity was an unprecedented willingness to allow himself to be pastored, ministered to and supported by family and others. And one very remarkable feature of his thinking about the Church during his last six months was that it was largely worked out in dialogue with a Jewish philosopher and theologian, to whom its writing-up was entrusted.[3] It is hard to find a parallel for this in Christian theology. There is also the envisaging of a group of five (see below), including a Muslim and a Jew, as something that might be seen as a sign of the ultimate fullness of the Church, and his engagement with the thought of each of them.

As for 'total God', there was no doubt that God was the pervasive concern during these months. The experiences of the pilgrimage concentrated and gave fresh symbolic and conceptual focus to what had always been central to his thought and conversation. As Deborah said in her tribute at his funeral, 'Quite early on I discovered that the best way to spend time with Dad was to talk about God. He could never get enough of that.'

This conversing about God, taking it as normal that one might not only relate all reality to God but also actually speak freely and inquiringly of who God is: that was, I think, the most amazing part of my years in Birmingham University as a young colleague of Dan. I never, even 30 years later, got used to the sense of freedom and intellectual adventure. We could start from anywhere – the Bible, physics, Dante, university politics, family life, liturgy, money, Hegel, religious education, the problem of evil or the perceptive comments of a local school caretaker who occasionally dropped in on us – and God could move effortlessly into the centre of conversation. Each Thursday morning, which we spent, year after year, in my flat in Birmingham just talking theology, was unpredictable. There could be hours or weeks of apparent detours from the book we eventually decided to write together, but always the golden thread was the reality and the sheer superabundance of meaning in God. The final six months of Dan's life brought a fresh dimension of such conversation, the unprecedented element in which was his experience of God on pilgrimage and the pressure of imminent death.

'So many genres are doing it!' – Varieties of Discourse

The problem with the density of the material for this book is that it has been quite a challenge to articulate it in digestible form. There was a moment in writing the book when we three authors real-ized something of the range and variety of what had been going on with Dan in our separate sets of conversations. We had each been working on our notes and met at Twin Lakes to see how they might all come together. As we shared the draft accounts we saw for the first time not only how many strands were woven together in Dan's theological and personal conversations during his final six months, but also how each of us had different mix-tures. Dan himself had recognized the issue of types of discourse in his exclamation about genres (quoted above) during one of our discussions. It was evoked by a conversation that had touched on theology, poetry, philosophy, scriptural commentary and herme-neutics, medicine, cosmology and his personal experience of God the previous night. Its recognition of multiplicity and distinctions was immediately followed by a desire for unity: 'I guess I'm just simple-minded: I need a glance of the whole.'

What we discovered was that with Peter the main discourses were narrative testimony, philosophy, theology (especially on God and Church), scriptural interpretation, science (especially to do with light and quantum measurement) and reflection on their intellectual autobiographies. With Deborah, the discourses included narrative testimony, scriptural interpretation, pastoral theology and practice, theology of priesthood and Church, psychotherapeutic theory and practice, poetry, literature, interpretation of dreams and symbols, and spirituality. With me there were narrative testimony, doctrinal theology, scriptural interpretation, poetry, education (especially regarding postgraduate supervision), inter-faith engagement, organizational and institutional policy, and reflections on his mode of thinking in comparison with those of others.

With all three of us there was much personal conversation too, and we found that Dan spoke frankly about matters on which he had been silent or very reticent before this. Little of that is included in this book, and in other respects too those final months can only be faintly represented here. It is not only that what was confidential should not be shared and that the abundance of conversations (during many of which we were not taking notes) defy adequate distillation. There is also the novelty of what we were witnessing in someone we knew well. For all the previous relationships we had with him, these months took us by surprise in many ways. The pilgrimage to Israel catalysed something in him that had no precedent. His powers of expression were stretched beyond their previous limits. He himself reached for many genres and discourses to try to convey his meaning, all of them drawn into the encompassing discourse of conversation.

It was moving to see him giving up control of the written form of his thought to others. He had always found writing difficult, and near the end he especially revelled in diagrams. In conversation he had always been in his element, but usually responsive rather than taking initiatives. There had been a curious passivity that generally let others set the agenda. But in these final months it was his agenda that led. It was not that he became less responsive, but there was a quiet determination that the implications of the pilgrimage, together with his core thought on the Church and related matters, had to be communicated as best they could.

Two statements from his final conversations with me point up the novelty.

Look at Micheal [O'Siadhail] – in his poetry there is always change, always movement. Give me a list of things to read in Micheal, especially in *Our Double Time*. He does *poetic reasoning*. I have become more of a poet and more of a storyteller in trying to express all this.

The poetry fed his oral storytelling. 'Storyteller' was not until then a term one would have associated with Dan, least of all storytelling in the genre of personal testimony. Yet this was in no competition with his diagramming and conceptualizing.

The possibility you mentioned earlier is an intriguing one: relating deeply to you and Deb and Jen is a way of living in refractions of the same ranges of things, so that they are always refracting on each other, each bringing to light something new in the others. That's the core significance of these discourses. The writing will be in the lives of people in the other situations Deb is in, you are in, the others in – not less valuable because it is not academic.

'Writing in the lives of people': here is both the integration of thought and life that was such a feature of his final months and also the key to his motivation in organizing those months around the communication of these discourses.

Concepts and Symbols

Abduction, attraction and fullness

This has been Coleridgian not Peircean. Through and through abductive: it lets be and lifts through being more and more completely attracted through the whole person and whole community and the whole universe. It is cosmic. The fullness of him who fills all in all: Ephesians 1. Romans 8. John. Luke 24 – hearts burning within us; the multiple openings of Scripture, hearts and minds, the tomb, opening to the whole world.

That interweaving of key concepts and biblical texts gives a sense of the scope of what Dan was exploring. Being drawn into the fullness of God and God's light, love and purposes was the deepest concern of his last six months.

What did he mean by 'abduction'? In ordinary speech the word can refer to 'abducting a child', in the sense of taking it away, kidnapping it. That is a way into the technical philosophical meaning as used by Dan. It is about how we come by fresh, imaginative thinking (in logical terms, something beyond deduction and induction). Dan's theological use puts the emphasis on being drawn into God's truth, 'abducted', so to speak, by God to where God wants us to be. It is therefore closely connected with the idea of divine attraction that recurs many times. And this attraction of our thinking by God towards God and towards the truth of God and of God's creation is into superabundant fullness – what he described above, following Coleridge, as 'a full life, total humanity, total Church, and total God'. As our thought and imagination are opened up to this endlessly rich reality we are stretched beyond whatever we have conceived so far.

In Paul's letter to the Ephesians, the culmination of chapter 1 (a dense chapter which Dan and I explored at length in thinking about praising God while writing *Living in Praise*, and again in preparation for Bible studies on Ephesians at the 2000 Anglican Communion Primates' Meeting in Porto) is the description of the Church as 'his body, the fullness of him who fills all in all' (Eph. 1.23). This is probably the most helpful single text to help grasp what is involved for him in a theology of the Church (ecclesiology). It has to be connected to God and to everything to which God relates. It is about a fullness of community with God, other people and the whole of creation. Clearly no actual community realizes this now, so there is a very strong emphasis on what God is attracting us into. There are likely to be many surprises, and we need to be open to all sorts of unexpected anticipatory signs of this ultimate community – for example, in the ways God has blessed Jewish and Muslim communities and has brought them into deep inter-faith relationships of love with Christians (see below). For Dan one of the most powerful signs of hope for the fulfilment of God's desire for the deepest communion with all humanity and creation was the Eucharist; it is the main everyday locus of attraction to God, a key instrument drawing us more deeply into God's love and wisdom.

There was an ongoing discussion between Dan and Peter about the best way to understand abduction. Peter was steeped in the American pragmatist philosopher C. S. Peirce,[4] who had a concept of abduction that emphasized the imaginative and rational human activity of reaching after new explanations and resolutions of problems and inventing fresh hypotheses. Dan brought Peirce into dialogue with Coleridge's use of abduction, which is more theological in emphasis (though he also took Peter's point that Peirce claimed that the ultimate source of our abductions is God the creator who is present in each true perception of the world). For Coleridge we are being attracted to God, 'drawn toward the true centre',[5] through particularity (Jesus Christ) and its relating universally (Holy Spirit).[6] We can be led into the truth (John 16.13), which means stretching the mind and imagination and often the will, too, since some truth is only known through action, above all through love.

Dan's overall conclusion on abduction was that Coleridge and Peirce are 'mutually fructifying . . . intersecting, correcting and enlarging', that we need to move beyond both of them, and that there is probably 'a need for a word other than "abduction" for "being drawn up and down and forward"'. In the absence of a single term, I suspect the phrase that best sums up his conception is 'being attracted into the fullness of God'.

Granulation

Granulation: it reaches down that deep. That's the redemptive side: that filtering goes all the way down, far more down than people realize . . . Letting be in a very real sense, something springing up. Letting one's own fullness come out.[9]

Dan liked to coin new theological terms. Granulation is a medical term for the process of healing from underneath a wound, as the tissue is knitted together afresh. He learned it towards the end of his life and used it frequently as a metaphor for God's ability to heal from deep within us. Whereas light is a more external image, granulation indicates something intrinsic to ourselves, and is more associated with the Spirit welling up within us like a spring of water (see below). He used it for the way Scripture can be internalized and work within us, for the embedding of deep meaning in the culture of a civilization, and for the wisdom that works within nature, and can be learnt from ants (as in Prov. 6.6; 30.24–25) – or from modern medicine.

Light and water: Symbols of attraction and granulation

It was utterly elemental – light, water, desire for both . . . It is attraction into divine light, into divine waters. There is the indefiniteness of powerful images, so powerful in relation to each other. In some amazing way the two things coalesce, I don't know how: being drawn into death is also being drawn into life.[10]

Light is undoubtedly the leading symbol of the conversations, closely accompanied by water. Light is above all the symbol of attraction, rooted in his Jerusalem experiences: in St George's Cathedral, a pillar of light; and, in the tunnel under the Western Wall, what he described as: '. . . amazing! . . . That whole place became a locus of light to me . . . to do with divine light, extremely powerful to such a degree that the whole place was irradiated by light, almost physically, the rocks shined.' Later he spoke of 'how the immensely attractive light of God emerges and how it has its effect. I had a happy night last night contemplating this: the joy of God's presence that confers joy and confers wellbeing.'

Water is associated both with the waters of baptism (symbolizing both cleansing from sin and dying in order to rise to new life) and with the Holy Spirit welling up from deep inside us (cf. John 4.13–14; 6.37–39). The headwaters of the River Jordan inspired a string of references to the significance of what 'bubbles up' from within and a rethinking of baptism in terms of the Spirit working continually in our depths. In his thought about attraction, granulation, light and water, he is dealing with one of the most complex issues in the history of theology, that of the relation of grace to nature, or divine initiative and human response, and is proposing a concept of their relationship that eliminates any notion of their being essentially in competition.

Measurement

How does that measurement take place? It is not a fixed system of measurement, but varies according to the significance of what happens, more like quantum measurement. There are not fixed units, as in Aristotelian philosophy of being, which is only suited to materiality. Beyond materiality there is the measurement of value, movement and significance: you are changing, what is being measured is changing, there are fluidities in the measuring. This has enormous significance for me: not fixing it in boxes. Boxes presume knowledge of what is coming into being – which you do not have. Early conversations with Peter about medieval Jewish philosophy offered some relevant material – post-box! There is no bottom to all this . . . In shorthand: this is about the Holy Spirit. This is what makes the Holy Spirit possible, that everything is not chopped up into boxes, so ongoing movement is possible. It is not the substance of the doctrine of the Holy Spirit, but makes the coast clear for it, helps conceive it. This leads back into the huge influence of Aristotle on Roman Catholic theology, always having predefined units: things must be this way and no other way.

The theme of measurement, originating in Dan's reflections on the measurement of the Holy Land and of Jerusalem,[7] is potentially vast. It suggests a fresh angle on a range of theological issues. One is the relation of theology and science, as in the potential for analogies to ideas of quantum measurement helping to free theology from over-rigid categories and criteria, and asking about the truth of Dan's suggestion that much theology is constricted by Aristotelian categories and their implied notions of measurement. Another issue is the Bible as a 'canon' (literally, 'measuring rod'): how its events or people or symbols might be used as measurements – this could open up fresh aspects of typology and figuration, and the use of the senses of Scripture; it also invites thinking about how the interpretation of Scripture in a specific situation, as an event in the Spirit, is a source of judgement. A third issue is how the very notion of measurement might relate to the superabundance of God's fullness, as suggested by a text referred to by Dan,

Ephesians 3.14–21, where the 'breadth and length and depth and height' of the love of Christ are set in relation to 'all the fullness of God'. Perhaps the most original of all his suggestions about measurement concerns Jesus walking (discussed below). I find this whole concept both strongly suggestive and very puzzling, and Dan did not have time to develop it coherently.

Sociopoiesis

What was happening? What was dripping as deeply as possible into people, welling up? It was about desire and water, the Spirit welling up to eternal life, uniting the water of baptism with the water you drink. What happens to transform someone from within like that? It was a regeneration. What is the effect on people *together*? There is a double effect: obviously on the individual, but how does it translate into something more? You must consistently resist individualization. You must look for *sociopoiesis* going on . . . How the group has to function develops over a long period, gradually . . . The description needs to reach down to elemental movements of the spirit, with beginnings in all sorts of inchoate desires, and it is significant how these get coherence. They have trajectories through rationality and through the affections, joining eventually in integrity, and all are raised by the divine, inward to the spirit, and permeating the person. It all impinges on a theory of the human – more, the socio-human – and all drawn into the divine light. See the Coleridge diagram: the schema of the human.[8]

Sociopoiesis (sometimes written socio-poiesis) – literally, 'making or creating the social' – is one of Dan's coinages (though it also appears in some sociological discussions) for the way sociality is formed. His concept of humanity is utterly social, as suggested by his coinage 'socio-human' above. This is essential to his understanding of the Church, which is called to realize the divine sociopoiesis in the world and to enable communities of many sorts to flourish. Dan made sociopoiesis the key concept in the last paper he wrote on ecclesiology, in which the diagram in

Chapter 2 above sums up his thinking on the dynamics of social creativity involving Church, nation and global society (see also below on the Church).

Walking

I've been for some time advocating a way of unfolding the Scripture texts by simply seeing Jesus walking, encountering Jesus walking. So there is not just frontal presentation of texts, but an increasing emphasis on not seeing the texts from an overarching standpoint (textual criticism, historical criticism, doctrine) but from the point of view of Jesus walking and encountering people. That is the viewpoint. Uppermost is watching Jesus encountering people. Scripture is formed by Jesus walking and encountering people, not by some overarching standpoint. There is question and answer. The text is taken up into conversation and interrogation, and there is no predicting where the conversation will end up. It is three-way, with Muslim, Christian and Jew; they are also being encountered. The Christian is to be like Jesus in conversation rather than saying: sign up to my faith statement. Jesus then is heard talking to Moses and Elijah too. This lifts the engagement beyond conventional questions. Each is saying: here we are, here is Jesus walking about among us.

The idea of Jesus walking – as a standpoint for interpreting the Gospels and for encounter with Jews and Muslims – might be seen as a continuation of the perspective of the Gospel writers: it draws us into an ongoing, open drama of the everyday, in which our contribution to the dialogue and action are shaping the plot. Its negative thrust is to undermine attempts at doctrinal, historical or theoretical overviews and judgements. It has positive implications for inter-faith engagement (see below) and for willingness to live immersed in history and its contingencies in a spirit of responsibility towards everyone we meet. And Jesus does not walk alone; he is with his disciples and open to many encounters and surprises beyond his own group.

Church and Beyond: The Edge of the Wind

> This is a definition of the Church: the formation of these people for other people.

Dan once described systematic theology to me as like an inner tube which could all be pulled through any one hole in it. I was not quite sure I understood about the inner tube, but it was clear what it meant as regards the different doctrines of theology. Take any one of them – God, creation, providence, sin, Jesus Christ, salvation, Church, eschatology – and in order to treat it adequately you would have to rethink all the others too. There was no doubt what was the leading doctrine in his final conversations: the Church. There was also no doubt that it was interconnected with all the others. What sort of ecclesiology results?

The answer is partly in Chapters 2 to 5, as given to Peter, and partly in his other writings. He positioned his final conversations with Peter between two of his books, *God's Ways with the World* and *Finding the Church*. The first is a broad theological framework for an ecclesiology, covering God, creation, the sciences, philosophy, poetry, a theological interpretation of modernity and his basic thinking on 'sociality', besides including sermons on a wide range of texts and occasions in the church year. The second is a collection of explorations in largely Anglican ecclesiology, springing from his engagement with the Church at parish, diocesan, national and international levels, and also including some sermons. I will not try to sum up an ecclesiology that deserves at least a monograph, but will comment on it with special reference to what emerged in his last conversations, and in particular with me.

> Scripture and Eucharist: consistent living in and presentation of the Church's life is terribly important to me, and constant exposure to that. That's why I really do rely very heavily on the Church. For me a lot of these things are like living in a house of abundance and simply drawing on that, rather than going for particular ways of thinking. The abundance is around them all the time.

These words evoke vividly the 'fullness of him who fills all in all' of Ephesians 1.23 as the ecology within which Dan lived and thought. His deep confidence in the God-centred reality of the Church was accompanied by constant critique of Church and society in the light of this. One of the most striking features of his thinking about the Church was his insistence that it is inseparable from, and utterly dedicated to, the flourishing of society, even defining ecclesiology as 'assembling all that is needed to provide the fullness of human society'. He spoke of the need for 'dialogue of the deepest sort between church society and civil society'. This was an area in which he looked to Coleridge, and also to Richard Hooker and Michael Ramsey. We reflected on the maxim of Bishop Graham Cray, which he introduced as a motto for the Anglican Evangelical theological college in Cambridge, Ridley Hall: 'Roots down, walls down'. Can the actual Church be so rooted in God, Scripture and Eucharist that it ceases to be self-protective, both sharing its abundance generously with society and receiving what society has to share with it?

But that picture of two-way exchange is far too simple. Dan was increasingly impressed by the value of diagrams, and he referred most often to the one he produced for his chapter in the book on Receptive Ecumenism.[9] This diagram allows for movement and exchanges in many different directions simultaneously, while keeping a central focus on sociopoiesis in its 'generation and shaping of relations'. It is Coleridgian in inspiration, and relates the Trinitarian God to the whole of creation and human life. The Church is vital but not easily separable from other social bodies, and Dan guides the reader along three trajectories in their interrelations – the nation, global society and the Church. The Church participates in the Spirit's generating ever-expanding orders of relation, and politics and commerce are as much a part of these as are covenant, Scripture and Eucharist. It is all oriented towards the attractive and attracting God who has created everything towards himself and works immanently as well as transcendently. The prime responsibility of the Church is to respond to this attraction, discerning it not only in obviously religious spheres but everywhere else too, and collaborating with others as they respond (or inviting and challenging those who do not).

The simultaneous relationships are taken up into its core forward-moving dynamic of 'temporal abduction' in response to God's 'abductive attraction'.[10] In other words, the whole of creation, through attraction with others to God, is being drawn by God's Spirit into the Kingdom of God.

In New Testament terms, this resonates especially with the Synoptic Kingdom of God, with Paul (for example Romans 8) and John (the drawing of all to Jesus, the Spirit leading into all truth and inspiring greater things than Jesus did); and one of Dan's favourite phrases for its movement is Coleridge's 'the Word through the Spirit'. This is the self-communication of God's 'I am', the Spirit-led re-creative ordering of life in all its aspects, opening up God's future through energizing love and wisdom. It is embodied in Jesus' ministry, transfiguration, last supper, death and resurrection and entered into through baptism and Eucharist, but it is perhaps most vividly and ordinarily seen in Jesus walking around the land encountering people in conversation and compassion.

It is no accident that the key diagram should have been elicited by thinking through Receptive Ecumenism. This is a collegial movement begun by Professor Paul Murray, founder of Durham University's Centre for Catholic Studies, a former student of Dan's and a long-time discussion partner. It emphasizes the need for Christian churches to learn from each other and is opening new ways of ecumenical study and collaboration. Dan attended its first major conference in January 2006 and entered fully into the debates. His paper and diagram combine deep rootedness in classic Christian Scripture and tradition with daring openness across boundaries, both among churches and between Church and society. He offers an ecclesiology to cope with the complexifying and transformation of boundaries necessary if ecumenism is to do justice to its responsibilities towards both Church and society.

But it is also no accident that in the same paper Dan links ecumenical and inter-faith engagement. In his final months he was far more concerned with Islam and Judaism than with intra-Christian relations. Scriptural Reasoning and the Cambridge Inter-Faith Programme were recurrent topics, and he had a great deal to say about *A Common Word Between Us and You*, the letter on love of God and love of neighbour sent by 138 Muslim leaders to the leaders of Christian churches in the month before he died, October 2007.[11] He reflected on how Jews, Christians and Muslims are 'knit together within the divine abundance' and how they relate to 'a single divine purpose':

> I realized in relation to Isra [Umeyye Isra Yazicioglu, a Muslim member of Scriptural Reasoning] and since through *A Common Word* that there is a deep awareness of an unbroken common word, not overthrown by the vicissitudes. I have a strong sense of the persistence of this superabundant light through all the traditions. You don't talk to Aref [Nayed] for more than five minutes before you are aware of that . . . It is not just things going on but growth, granulation going on that is happening at the most basic levels of light and at the greatest levels – with God as well as humankind. That's a tall order, a genuine healing happening within, within God as leaders join in deep contemplation of God; but that there is something happening with God is pretty well unquestionable. It is a knitting together in the divine that goes beyond anything anyone has dreamed of. These are not movements at one remove from God, but movement within God. I don't know how that would go down with absolutist Muslims or Christians. But this occurs to me more strongly: healing is necessarily at the level of a common word, with healing at the topmost level. This is difficult for people to accept. If healing is at the most basic underground level, why not at the topmost level? It must be thought in terms of love, and overlaying and knitting together of strands that have been sundered. The most urgent thing is how to make this effective at the level of the common word. What needs to happen for this engagement to go more deeply? That's a big, big idea. It requires people to engage at a much more profound level than they are ready to . . . Rowan [Williams] must take it fully seriously.[12] *It is a matter of growing something from beneath, the Spirit welling up in the group.* It is such a challenge, an unmissable opportunity.

This and other conversations explored the limits of what 'Church' might mean, using the case of inter-faith engagement.

To recognize that close inter-faith fellowship participates some-how in the divine abundance across the boundaries of our faith communities, yet without removing deep, enduring differences about how God is identified and responded to: that is a tension that is especially sharp in relation to the Church. If the Church is the body of Christ, 'the fullness of him who fills all in all' (Eph. 1.23), how do we as Christians hold together that 'all' and the specificity of the body of Christ? If the discernment of 'Church' is closely tied to discernment of God's fullness and abundance, and that fullness is found in some inter-faith engagement, what are the boundaries of the Church? It is not that there are no boundaries, no limits to what God is understood to fill; but we have no over-view of them, and may be frequently surprised at the movement of the Spirit 'welling up in the group'. To change the metaphor from water to air: who can identify the edge of the wind?

For Dan, inter-faith fellowship in depth came late, the culmi-nation of what might be called his gift for 'collegial friendship', which developed especially from his Birmingham years. It might be described as friendship with a strong element of joint theo-logical vocation. It was usually just with one other person, and Dan had many such relationships. There were also groups in the Church and the academy, with an especially important and long-term constellation of relationships within the Society for the Study of Theology, where his leadership was formative over many years. Scriptural Reasoning added a new dimension, as he became close to Jews and Muslims; and in his active retirement in Cambridge he, unusually, took some initiatives in forming some significant collegial groups, where intensive conversation happened.

In the final six months there was a further intensity to these, and part of the integration of life and thought was through conversa-tion within and about these friendships. Looking back over notes from that period I am especially struck by repeated references in conversation with me to three friendships we shared together: with Aref Nayed, Micheal O'Siadhail and Peter Ochs. Indeed, several times he spoke of the five as a group, which needed to meet, and on one occasion he even named December as the best time for us to come together. We never did all meet (he died in November), not even at his funeral – one could not come. But this group – Jewish, Christian and Muslim – perhaps even in the very fact of not having actually met, was a sign for him of the fullness of God, a God-centred community of collegial friendship that anticipates the ultimate fullness of the Kingdom of God – and in the meanwhile is a catalyst for signs that are fuller and richer realizations of the love and wisdom of God.

There is one further element to be added concerning his relationship to the Church during this time – his own moving statement about his vocation as a priest:

> I've been content ever since the onset of this cancer to be drawn into death, but I don't take this negatively at all: it is also being drawn into life and the two are closely tied together. I don't know what to make of it, but I have known since the onset of the cancer that it might lead to death and that much depends on the quality of life it brings forth in the meantime. That gives me not a little peace in all this. There is the prospect of death, but what big deal is that? It is a contingent death, but there is nothing fearful in that – there is also the promise of life. In some deep way I don't understand there is *a coming of life in death* . . . What I'm indicating is: there is a very close affinity of life and death. Perhaps I'm being a sort of sign of attraction, going ahead of you into the mystery, an attraction not into anything clear and unambiguous but into a light that is the mystery of death and life, and therein God. It is the fulfilment of my priestly vocation.

God, the Spirit and the Future of Theology

'This is about the Holy Spirit.' That was said in the middle of a discussion of measurement, but it is equally appropriate to many other themes Dan was exploring. God pervades the conversations: he spoke of 'my almost insatiable concern for God, not just for knowledge of God, but a more insatiable thirst again than that'. The Spirit of God is the most frequently recurring theme. Key imagery is characteristically related to the Spirit: thirst and water, light, fullness, overflowing abundance, life, walking, newness.

I was reminded of Dan's fascination over many years with

beginning an understanding of the Trinity from the Spirit. This went back to his Birmingham days and recurs in his writings at various points since then. In the final six months it returns and in the conversations with me is more prominent even than those related to Church – and, of course, the latter are also inseparable from the Spirit. More fundamentally, the Spirit is inseparable from the Word, and Coleridge's 'Word in the Spirit' recurred as the best way into

the full richness of the Trinitarian life . . . What is the heart of the Trinity? I've always thought, liked and hoped that it is the heart of the energizing of the light of God. Whenever it is definite it is immediately transcended. It is damaged by definition. Defining has its place, thinking as rigorously as possible, but you must allow yourself to be humbled by the reality. Definitions are always humbled by the immense depth of reality.

This especially requires a Spirit-led approach to Scripture:

It is amazing testimony to the New Testament: each Gospel tries to cope differently with the superabundance. We need a commentary on Scripture that acknowledges and celebrates the fullness and that is itself drawn into all sorts of creativity, to do greater things – as Coleridge does. We must do justice to this fullness in the Spirit, not just tell about it. So commentary must be very different. Ideally it is preaching people into the celebration, the engagement with the Spirit. The fullness of God! If you could get a level of engagement with the Spirit with the text in which people are taken up into the engagement in the Spirit, that would be extraordinary. There is a sense in which engagement with the Spirit is always primary, the moving Spirit of God. That is the most astonishing thing in the New Testament. It is the principal area where people resist. The Spirit is utterly with Scripture, utterly with adoration, utterly with the whole tiered universe. The endless attractiveness of this light and love: what we are drawn into by grace and beauty, by the glory in the face of Christ.

The ramifications of this approach go in many directions, the Spirit being associated with community (sociopoiesis), transformation, speaking, rejoicing and dying. This is not the place to explore those further, but in conclusion I will briefly draw out four pointers for the future of theological thinking.

The first is the constant recurrence together of Scripture and the classic doctrines (especially those of God, creation, Jesus Christ, the Holy Spirit, Church and eschatology). Dan is not doing conventional systematic theology (if there is such a thing), but in his conversations with me is taking for granted what may be called its deep grammar: a constant interplay between the Bible, the doctrines and a range of contemporary questions and discourses. At its simplest this suggests a basic condition for fruitful, educated theological thinking: competence in understanding Scripture, the doctrines and a range of current disciplines.

The second and third are topics of a 'theology and . . .' kind, which is a type that has multiplied remarkably in recent decades. Dan has a good deal to say about theology and science (there is even more about this in his conversations with Peter Ochs) and also about theology and other faiths. On theology and science, besides the topics already discussed in previous chapters he also showed a fascination for the way Micheal O'Siadhail's poetry engages with science:

He has the scope of Dante, and knows some science. I feel grossly deficient in science. It is too vast and indeterminate. The only thing one can do is to go into it with a good will and explore . . . Micheal has a sensitivity that is quite remarkable, together with real thinking. It is a way of granulation, how Coleridge and Micheal have worked.

Likewise, he was intrigued by Aref Nayed's having degrees in engineering and philosophy of science as well as hermeneutics, and what this meant for his theology as a Muslim.

On theology and other faiths, at one point he laid out a central problem starkly:

I want to affirm both: 'This is God's providence: God actually wants there to be Muslims in Britain now'; and: 'God wants all people to rejoice in his Son and in the Holy Spirit.' Can these be held together? Yes, and they must interpenetrate. They must be knit together. It is a matter of abduction seen in Trinitarian terms. The supervening thing is divine abundance and therefore gratitude for being drawn up into a single divine purpose. It is a mystery, like the ending of Romans 9—11. This is a theme that needs to be followed through, and it is quite exciting: abduction out of the superabundance of the divine. There is one God, the divine is non-divisive. Barth's great contribution to the unity of God is his doctrine of election . . . What is there still to come in terms of divine presence? Partly it spins into the question of present and future. The eschatological aspect is underestimated. I can't get away from the fact that a lot more is to be said about how things and people are knit together in the divine abundance – an indefinite resource of human wholeness, and wholeness for the universe too. What is it that people are growing into? There is a far more profound human integrity than we have yet glimpsed. What is it that grows a good, whole human being and a good society?

That is a set of undeveloped prompts for further thinking, but it is clear that, for him, Paul's letter to the Romans, chapters 9 to 11, was the most remarkable and creative wrestling with the question of fundamental theological differences in the Bible. It sets the core challenge for inter-faith theology in the twenty-first century. As in Paul, the central dynamic is being led by the Spirit deeper and deeper into the mystery of God:

For me *A Common Word* is knitting and overlaying traditions without the supposition that they are at loggerheads. What is the profounder level of commonness? What is the intensity within the extensity? The challenge and excitement of this! There is something to rest in; there is a persistent sense I have: we have not yet learnt to *rest* in that which is most fundamental and common to us all. How do we reach deeper into the commonness? Only by going into the profoundest source of all, without prematurely naming it. The Lord and God of Sinai, I am that I am, is not just simply: that means you're saying you're

God. There is an indefinite prolongation about this. People leap in with 'God'. What if this is something fathomless? I'd like to hear Aref for an hour on Allah, Rowan [Williams] for an hour on the Christian God, Peter on Adonai Elohim. That would give not a bad set of study items to begin with. It is hard to get away from the need for serious, considered study at the beginning of this. That would be very exciting. Have that December meeting.

Much of Dan's fundamental thinking, when it was not focused on God and other doctrines, was concerned with theology and science (especially in his Birmingham period) and with theology and other faiths (especially in Princeton and Cambridge). The two came together in the last six months in suggestive ways, opening them up further as leading themes for the present century. 'That December meeting' was to be his attempt to go further on the inter-faith front, and he saw it needing

> to probe deeply and shift levels of interchange, working on primary texts that intersect with each other. Collegiality needs to open up and spread around, and there needs to be some analysis of how it has happened . . . My deepest desire for the Five is: to get under the surface of the disjunctions, discern how to move bit by bit. In the conversation with Peter yesterday we explored how jointly to enter into the text more fully.

It was a vision of hope, with recognition of the patient, detailed work needed to realize it.

The fourth pointer was his recurrent reflection on modes of thinking in theology and related areas. Micheal O'Siadhail had sent Dan poems from the forthcoming book he was working on at the time, called *Tongues*.[13] Dan was very much taken by them and spoke at length about their poetic exploration of how language works, especially grammar.

> That is a way of concentrating the multiplicity . . . There is something very interesting about grammar – bringing things into focus, linguistic intensity. Micheal knows the grammar of

many languages. It is a linguistic parallel to approaching the divine intensity. It amazing what he is doing – it's all real, linguistically, in Japanese and other languages.

He related this multiple linguistic intensity to Moses and God's 'I am who I am' in Exodus 3.14: 'indefinitely full of implications, constantly generative . . . The Trinity offers appropriate categories and coordination for multiple intensity.' He also reflected on the mode of thinking in my recently published book *Christian Wisdom: Desiring God and Learning in Love*,[14] seeing it as a 'huge act of coordination' and finding in it 'an abductive structure'. Then he drew a contrast:

> Peter and I are different from you: we work on the theory of how the coordination happens. Transposed into linguistic terms that involves a theoretical coordination of language. You can also do this in a grammatical way, as Micheal does, or a realistic way, as you do in the wisdom book, plumbing different ways of coordinating life in the world. Peter's, which I largely share, is looking for the conditions for it all coming together, conditions for the possibility of this – somewhat like idealism? . . . Each (yours, Micheal's, Peter's and mine) needs to be worked on more and made more explicit. All are concerned with intensity, maximum concentration.

Yet, for all the theorizing and seeking of transcendental conditions, there was also the simplicity of walking and sitting like Jesus, and conversation as the most common and valuable form of theology. Near the end he spent a long time on 2 Corinthians 4.5ff.:

> For we do not proclaim ourselves; we proclaim Jesus Christ as Lord and ourselves as your slaves for Jesus' sake. For it is the God who said, 'Let light shine out of darkness', who has shone in our hearts to give the light of the knowledge of the glory of God in the face of Jesus Christ. But we have this treasure in clay jars, so that it may be made clear that this extraordinary power belongs to God and does not come

from us. We are afflicted in every way, but not crushed; perplexed, but not driven to despair; persecuted, but not forsaken; struck down, but not destroyed; always carrying in the body the death of Jesus, so that the life of Jesus may also be made visible in our bodies. For while we live, we are always being given up to death for Jesus' sake, so that the life of Jesus may be made visible in our mortal flesh. So death is at work in us, but life in you.

This is lived as dialogue, as servants, friends, of the facing Lord. There is a triple hermeneutic for the three traditions, with Jesus walking between the traditions, not just the property of one: Jesus is Jewish and is a Muslim prophet. So he is well suited to walking among them, hosting a conversation, not closing down things. Paul is not about being in control, but about dying: he is carrying around the dying of Jesus – including his farewell discourses. *Nekrosis* [Greek: dying, death]. Jesus' walking about Galilee culminated in the Last Supper – walking, meals, transfiguration, his death relativized in the presence of light. I would not want to lose sight of the hardness of it. It is not just about light, but being hard pressed, bewildered, hunted, struck down. It is hard: the demands of walking with Jesus are considerable.

Yet 'hardness' was never the overall impression you had with Dan: no matter how difficult things were. There was always a much deeper sense of the sheer joy and wonder at the attractiveness and energy of the light; the water of life 'bubbling up'. As he put it,

It is attraction into divine light, into divine waters. There is the indefiniteness of powerful images, so powerful in relation to each other. In some amazing way the two things coalesce, I don't know how: being drawn into death is also being drawn into life.

How precious is your steadfast love, O God!
All people may take refuge in the shadow of your wings.

They feast on the abundance of your house,
And you give them drink from the river of your delights.

For with you is the fountain of life;
In your light we see light. (Psalm 36.7–9)

Happy are those whose strength is in you,
in whose heart are the highways to Zion.

As they go through the valley of Baca
they make it a place of springs;
the early rain also covers it with pools.

They go from strength to strength;
the God of gods will be seen in Zion. (Psalm 84.4–6)

Notes

1 All unacknowledged quotations in this chapter are the words of Dan Hardy in conversation with David Ford.

2 *The Collected Works of Samuel Taylor Coleridge, Shorter Works and Fragments II*, ed. by H. J. Jackson and J. R. de J. Jackson, Routledge, Bollingen Series LXXV, London: Routledge and Princeton: Princeton University Press, 1995, p. 1385.

3 He also asked Peter Ochs to preach at his funeral.

4 See Peter Ochs, *Peirce, Pragmatism and the Logic of Scripture*, Cambridge: Cambridge University Press, 1998.

5 For references and discussion, see Daniel W. Hardy, 'Harmony and Mutual Implication in the *Opus Maximum*', in Jeffrey W. Barbeau, ed., *Coleridge's Assertion of Religion: Essays on the Opus Maximum*, Leuven, Paris, Dudley, MA: Peeters, 2006, especially pp. 50ff.

6 Hardy ('Harmony', p. 52) concludes: 'In that "being drawn", human beings are most truly enabled to affirm themselves and the order of all things, as they are illuminated in Reason and directed in love toward 'all things both great and small, for the dear God who loveth us, He made and loveth all' (from Coleridge's poem, 'The Rime of the Ancient Mariner'). This "abduction" is indeed a maximal insight, a fitting conclusion, both methodological and realistic, to Coleridge's lifelong pursuit of the mutual implication of all things in the Logos and the Spirit.'

7 These are biblical themes. One especially fascinating text is the Book of Ezekiel; Dan discussed chapter 47 at some length.

8 Dan Hardy on what happened at the headwaters of the Jordan.

9 Daniel W. Hardy, 'Receptive Ecumenism: Learning by Engagement', in Paul D. Murray, ed., *Receptive Ecumenism and the Call to Catholic Learning: Exploring a Way for Contemporary Ecumenism* (Oxford: Oxford University Press, 2008), p. 434. The diagram is reproduced above, Chapter 2, p. 48.

10 On these see 'Receptive Ecumenism', pp. 436ff.

11 For the text of the letter and the remarkable record of responses, see www.acommonword.com.

12 Rowan Williams did in fact in July 2008 send the fullest response to date, his letter *A Common Word for the Common Good* (see www.acommonword.com).

13 Forthcoming, Bloodaxe Books, 2010.

14 Cambridge University Press, 2007.

PART FOUR

7

Farewell Discourses

Deborah Hardy Ford in conversation with Daniel W. Hardy

In a sense, the whole of this book has been a series of farewell discourses: my father's 'parting theology' set in the context of his lifetime pilgrimage and theological inquiry; but the following is an account of conversations he and I had that were more specifically about his dying and the meaning this held for him. They took place mostly during the last week of his life, when he 'set his face to Jerusalem'. It was the week that he finished dictating the contents of this book, when Peter was able to say for the first time: 'I've got the book: Dan has finished it.'[1]

If he had been able to write the book himself (as he would have loved), it would have been a very different one, not only in genre, but perhaps in content, too: perhaps his ability to 'see' the immensity and attractiveness of God's light – and all the transformations that went with it – would not have happened if he had not been beginning to die.

His pilgrimage to the Holy Land was the beginning of his final pilgrimage. Along with his diagnosis (two weeks after his return to Cambridge), he was given seven to eight months to live: without treatment, it would only be weeks. 'That's the minimum,' he said. 'Seven to eight months is the absolute minimum,' and he began to fight it.

I asked, 'What's it like to realize suddenly that your life is limited? That it's going to be shorter than you expected?'

'It's strange,' he replied. 'I thought I'd have another ten years or so – but if that's the way it is, so be it . . . It's in God's hands.

Years ago I became very aware of that, that life is in God's hands: we are here for as long as he needs us to be.'

'You don't believe in a God who takes life away, do you?' I asked, horrified.

'No, but I do believe in a God who gives us life and purpose, and that we are given as long as we need here to fulfil that purpose.'

In learning that his life was more limited than he had thought, time heightened and thickened. It became 'double time': 'Every minute still so full, so precious, a furious intensity of knowing it ends . . .'[2]

All I could pray was, 'Lord, have mercy.'

He savoured the moments he had with people in between treatments and his growing need for rest. His deep desire was to get to 'the Lake' (his summer home in Connecticut) and to gather with his family there, and he underwent radical surgery and radiotherapy in order to do so. This last time, exhausted from the toll of the treatment, together with the journey, it was wonderful to see him gradually coming back to life there. One of his favourite things was simply to lie stretched out on the grass, taking it all in: the sky; the water; the light and the interplay of colours; the breezes and the scents, and all our faces with their to and fro of laughter and conversation . . . There was a new sense of play and freedom about him. He said of it, 'It was a wonderful summer: it's all I could possibly have hoped for.' But it was agony too, and he found any sense of conflict or tension increasingly difficult. There was a new and greater sense of both receptivity (passivity) and pro-activity in him.

We spoke of theodicy and of the deep irony that his brain – one of his greatest gifts – was the very part of him that had become vulnerable and was being 'attacked'. He spoke of the deep cost of seeing: the more he saw the light, the more it exposed, and the more he was aware of the terrible darkness and resistance to the light; of our failure to let the potential for the goodness created in creation actually come into being and grow into its fullness of being/life in us: betraying the goodness entrusted to us – 'the infinite potential of the world' (his words).

I am more powerfully aware of 'wrongness' than before: it's not localized, but all humanity. What now bothers me is not who has it 'right' or 'wrong' (Jews, Christians or Muslims) – but that the world is sinking . . . That strikes me hard: that by failing to be attracted to the light we are slipping into darkness. It's a frightful failure in living up to the light: in responding appropriately and bearing the light. It's not a matter of trying to live up to the light itself as angels (as if we could!), but to live up to it fully on our own level. In light of this light I see clearly what we are not doing; we need a renewed attention and engagement with the light and a willingness to review everything as a result: to reach through to the light through what we do, to be found *by* the light by what we do is a better way to put it. It means taking worship seriously: taking the text of Scripture more seriously than we do and being found by what is happening in Scripture.

He even wondered if this vivid, costly seeing was what had caused his brain tumour. He described a moment in the tunnel under the old city wall of Jerusalem, the crucible where so much tension has been focused and held over the years – the place of the Holy of Holies – where he was acutely aware of this as a pain in his head (and although the tumour could have affected his perception of light, it never caused him any physical pain). No-one will ever know.

In any case, no matter how much we didn't want any of this to be happening, we were strangely aware of something powerfully redemptive taking place in our midst: we were being led deeper into the paradox of the cross: its glory, its mystery, its 'crosslight'.[3]

I have known since the onset of the cancer that it might lead to death and that much depends on the quality of life it brings forth in the meantime . . . Being drawn into death is also being drawn into life: there is a close affinity between the two. Death is relativized in the presence of light. Perhaps I'm being a sort of sign of attraction, going ahead of you into the mystery, an attraction not into anything clear and unambiguous but into a light that is the mystery of death and life, and therein God. It is the fulfilment of my priestly vocation.[4]

It was about being fully alive in his dying: possible, perhaps, because 'in his living he had begun to die'.[5] He was not frightened of his tumour or of dying. He even found it very difficult when certain letters arrived saying 'We're praying for a miracle.' He said it wasn't right – 'How can we expect to be excused from our humanity?' He saw cancer and suffering as 'normality' in the world as it is now – that 'tumours happen and need to be received'. And he believed strongly it was part of the priestly vocation to teach and show people how to die well.

I asked, 'How do you reconcile the fact that you want to live and fight the tumour for as long as possible, and being peaceful and ready to die when the time comes?'

'You can't reconcile them,' was his reply. 'The task is to be open and available to be used by God for as long as he wants.'

He was describing a letting go – 'a caring less which means my caring more'[6] – consistent with his whole theology of attraction:

Something about the light is its openness and not being exclusive: its being open is inherent to it. We can't contain or possess the light – however much we might want to or try to. Remember YHWH, 'I am who I am and I shall be who I shall be . . .' We cannot grasp hold: that's the mystery of entering and going deeper into relationship with God: it's not about loss or restriction, but gain. What's best for God is best for me (and us), too.

And no matter how much I wanted to cling on to him, a deep-down part of me recognized something – the truth – in what he was saying.

I remember, when we moved to Birmingham (I was five) and went to a new church, how surprised I was that lots of people started coming up and calling him 'father', and how indignant I felt about it: this was my father – not theirs! But I learned fairly quickly that it was OK: there was so much of him that there was plenty of him to go round. He could be fatherly ('God-fatherly') to many, many people all at the same time and still be utterly mine.

During his illness there was a profound transformation within him: a deep movement from a philosophy and theology founded fundamentally on remedy to one springing from sheer praise:

> The world has huge potential that it's sunk away from . . . But it's important not to focus on the remedial – but to focus on the huge *potential*: God's goodness and Spirit at work in and among us! It's easy to get stuck in the blockages rather than focusing on the wonder and glory and vision of God and getting swept up and caught up in it . . . It's not a matter of us working out 'how'; it's about 'letting be' in a very real sense, something springing up and letting one's own fullness come out . . . Something is waiting to happen and I want to see what it is!

It was a profound six months accompanying him in his facing his death, seeing him get better as a result of the treatments, but yet knowing he was never going to get fully better – and especially, when the moment came, when it was obvious to those around him that earlier symptoms were returning and worsening.

Gently helping him to face the reality of his deterioration was not easy, yet he was deeply trusting and accepted help with huge dignity, humility and courage. Sometimes he was not clear enough to be able to realize how bad things really were for him, but he was always grateful for his 'reality checks'.[7]

I asked, 'You've done so well for so long, Dad, I wonder what it's going to feel like when they say they can't do any more?'

And he replied, 'I don't know: I hope it will be to be thankful. I don't want to fall into a slough of despond, because this time has been wonderful. The main job is simply to articulate the wonder and be thankful for what has happened . . . and to have articulated enough.'

Further consultation with the oncologist confirmed that the tumour had returned and that it was unlikely any more treatment would help. It had gone so well, and he had lived so intensively and well in the extra time it had given him, that he couldn't really understand why he couldn't simply have it all again: neurosurgery, radiotherapy, chemotherapy, whatever it took . . . But that wasn't an option, no matter how much he wanted it to be. It was explained to him gently, 'Your brain can only take so much, you know . . .' (Indeed it was easy to underestimate quite what he had already been through.)

In the car on the way home, we began to explore the possibility that he might be entering a new stage – a move from the more physical to the more spiritual in preparation for the fullness that was yet to come; and we remembered Paul's 'and yet'.[8]

> Therefore, since it is by God's mercy that we are engaged in this ministry, we do not lose heart . . . For we do not proclaim ourselves; we proclaim Jesus Christ as Lord . . . For it is the God who said, 'Let light shine out of darkness', who has shone in our hearts to give the light of the knowledge of the glory of God in the face of Jesus Christ. But we have this treasure in clay jars, so that it may be made clear that this extraordinary power belongs to God and does not come from us. We are afflicted in every way, but not crushed; perplexed, but not driven to despair; persecuted, but not forsaken; struck down, but not destroyed; always carrying in the body the death of Jesus, so that the life of Jesus may also be made visible in our bodies . . . So we do not lose heart. Even though our outer nature is wasting away, our inner nature is being renewed day by day. For this slight momentary affliction is preparing us for an eternal weight of glory beyond all measure, because we look not at what can be seen but at what cannot be seen; for what can be seen is temporary, but what cannot be seen is eternal.[9]

It coincided almost simultaneously with the ending of his pilgrimage narrative as he had dictated it to me.

Soon after this, he wanted to talk about his dying. To me (as a hospital chaplain), this felt both very familiar and yet very unfamiliar ground. I was used to talking with people facing death, and although it felt slightly different with my own father (the one to whom I had turned for help in talking about difficult things many times), I was not afraid.

'I wonder what preparing to die might be about for you?' I asked.

'It's difficult to say; I've never done it before: its uncharted territory,' was his reply. 'What about for you?'

'Dad – if it's uncharted territory for you, what do you think it is for me?!'

But I began to imagine and wondered what my (and his) vision or metaphors for heaven might be (feast, dance, heavenly city and so on), although that was not really what it was about for him: 'I don't really find them helpful: for me, it's more about light.'

He began to tell me about times during the last month when he had woken 'out of the blue' in the middle of the night, usually for several hours at a time:

> Moments of peace and revelation when all sorts of things can come right, just 'given' moments – not anything in my control or that I could make happen, but they've been astonishing . . . not in their brilliance or anything like that, but in their benevolence and the joy they bring. They're pure grace . . . I simply savour them and let them linger.

After a few moments he went on:

> They're not particular memories – there's nothing tangible about them at all – nothing material, but they are pure grace and joy. It's been happening for the last month or so – never before. It's difficult not to imagine they're a hinterland, a threshold place, and it's just fine. It's not anything you can grasp at, but a wondrous kind of rest . . . and it leaves a surplus during the day. It's a wonderful resourcing to help cope with the difficult things. If anything, the issue is how to get those moments embedded in you deeply.

This was the moment when I suddenly realized that my father had started to die (despite scans showing no change in his condition at all).

For a moment he began to speak about the transformation of his desire through someone else, someone I knew and had told him about who was also dying: 'Think of Harry: it doesn't matter to him if he lives or dies, does it?'

'And you?' I asked.

No: I sorted that out a long time ago; it's not in my control. Right at the beginning of this [cancer] it was very clear to me that I'll be here as long as God needs me or wants me to be, and in that sense it doesn't matter physiologically. I'll be here as long as I can contribute something – and that's not up to me. There's something very tentative about my continued life here and it's not functional; but there's some connection between this contingency and beyond. I have a continuous awareness of God's glory, and to be given the chance to articulate it is the beginning of the next life. I only wish I could show people more of it . . .

It reminded me of Etty Hillesum (whose diary and letters contained her own 'farewell discourses' written during the months leading up to her death in Westerbork in 1943, and which I was re-reading at the time):

I now realize, God, how much you have given me. So much that was beautiful and so much that was hard to bear. Yet whenever I showed myself ready to bear it, the hard was directly transformed into the beautiful. And the beautiful was sometimes harder to bear, so overpowering did it seem . . .

[Then from within the camp]

Most people are deadened here . . . I want to be the thinking heart of the barracks . . . to be able to say 'Life is beautiful.' A camp needs a poet, one who experiences life there, even there, as a bard and is able to sing about it . . . There is no poet in me; just a little piece of God that might grow into some poetry. So I shall wait patiently until the words have grown inside me, the words that proclaim how good and beautiful it is to live in your world, oh God, despite everything we human beings do to one another . . . You have made me so rich, oh God, please let me share your beauty with open hands.[10]

For my father it was about living up to the light: being worthy of the glory shone in our hearts. He said, 'It's all about love. I want to show people, more than tell them: to try to awaken it in other people – not from outside – but from deep within them. That's what "walking with Jesus" is: look at all he did, all those "love statements" opening out of his meetings with things and people.'

> After Jesus had spoken these words, he looked up to heaven and said, 'Father, the hour has come; glorify your Son so that the Son may glorify you . . . I have made your name known to those whom you gave me . . . Now they know that everything you have given me is from you; for the words that you gave to me I have given to them, and they have received them and know in truth that I come from you; and they have believed that you sent me. I am asking on their behalf . . . because they are yours. All mine are yours, and yours are mine; and I have been glorified in them . . . Holy Father, protect them in your name that you have given me, so that they may be one as we are one . . . But now I am coming to you, and I speak these things in the world so that they may have my joy made complete in themselves . . . Sanctify them in the truth; your word is truth. (John 17.1–17)[11]

Things intensified still further as my father 'set his face' to his actual dying and to the heart of 'Jerusalem'. Our relationship and roles as priests, father and daughter criss-crossed, and, at times, it felt as if it would be unbearable. And yet as his illness progressed, he was somehow increasingly able to bear his lot. As Etty Hillesum also wrote from Westerbork:

> That is what is so desperate about this place: most people are not able to bear their lot and they load it onto the shoulders of others. And that burden is more likely to break one than one's own lot.[12]

On Palm Sunday (the week *before* he had set off on his pilgrimage to the Holy Land) I had had the following dream:

> Daniel[13] has been taken hostage, and I am desperate to find him. He is in serious danger and may well die. I need to see him before – and in case – he does. It is against all the odds, but

I finally manage to find him: we are suddenly face to face on our own in a sort of conservatory room. Danger is all around and we both know that this might be the last time we see each other. I have a terrible pain in me – it feels almost unbearable as we give each other a huge hug and hold tight. I try to say, 'Whatever happens, I love you so much: you've been such a gift to me . . .', and I am surprised that I can feel Daniel giving some strength and support back to me, as he holds me tight; and I know how much he loves me and how precious I am to him. We just stay there, holding each other close. We don't know what is going to happen.

Somehow my father was able to prepare and resource us for his departure.[14] One day he said to David (they too had been talking about the passage from 2 Corinthians 4 quoted above):

> Paul is not talking about being in control, but about dying: he is carrying around the dying of Jesus – including his farewell discourses. *Nekrosis*. Jesus' walking about Galilee culminated in the Last Supper – walking, meals, transfiguration, his death relativized in the presence of light. I would not want to lose sight of the hardness of it: the demands of walking with Jesus are considerable.

But with me, he was less open about how difficult he found it; he was somehow able to bear his lot, drawing on the wisdom and strength of the whole Christian tradition that resourced him so deeply, so that he could be there for me, too. And at no point was there ever any sense of escapism or fantasy. He was facing things in a way that plunged us all deeper into reality. Accompanying him in his walking with Jesus meant walking through Gethsemane to death.

The backdrop for the drama that held and sustained us all within its 'bigger time' was the church year, in which we found ourselves re-membered within the wider history of the Christian drama: from his departure for the Holy Land on Easter Day through diagnosis and surgery in Ascensiontide; the months of reprieve through Pentecost and Trinity ('ordinary time'), right up to his death in All Saints Tide.

A few years before he died my father had written, 'All-told, it has been a wonderful life, unexpected in so many ways: not without its disappointments and hardships, but deeply fulfilling . . .'[15] A few weeks before he died he said, 'I am so grateful for all that's happened through all of this – I wouldn't have not had it – I've seen and understood things I'd never been able to before . . . And my role has been to articulate the wonder as fully as I can . . . I only wish I could show people more of it.'

That's when I suddenly recognized what he was saying: that if *this* was his task, to articulate praise, then it could never be completed – in this life or the next – only ever begun and then carried on throughout all eternity. He said, 'This continuous awareness of God's glory and being given the chance to articulate it is the beginning of the next life . . . When I die I hope that I am *praising*: that's what I want my last words to be.'

He had a profound sense of gratitude and of the importance of expressing gratitude; as he put it, 'Intensity has its consequences for me. My next job is to write a statement of gratitude.' And again one day, as we were waiting in the Oncology clinic at Addenbrooke's hospital: 'It's a wonderful place this hospital. I want to write and tell them and thank them. They must hear so many complaints: they need some passionate affirmation.'

A week before he died, my father took a sudden turn for the worse. It was his seventy-seventh birthday, and he was just able to join us in the evening as we celebrated him and his life together, but from then on he was increasingly weak and sleepy.

It was deep in autumn and somehow the light and colours were more beautiful than ever that year. He loved to sit or lie as close to the window as he could, often with his eyes shut, soaking in the glorious autumnal sunlight and hues.

We reflected on what a week it had been: so much had happened since we'd last really been able to talk. Then he said,

I think I probably am dying . . . So letting love grow between us between now and the end is what matters now: just as it is in life as a preparation for death anyway . . . and whatever happens, it's important that we've declared the intention.

Things became clearer and simpler, more refined in their complexity. 'It's all about passion, you know, that's what it's all about: love, passion, the ultimate simplicity and the ultimate complexity.' 'The ultimate intensity and the ultimate extensity' (I can almost hear him adding).

We wondered what his dying might mean now (in this stage): we talked of blessing: of his night-time 'blessings' (the times when he would wake full of wonder, peace and joy), of the story of Jacob on his deathbed blessing his sons, and of what his own farewell blessings might be for each of his loved ones.

That was the day when we talked about light and colour: 'This light I've talked about and see infused in people and between people and things isn't white light, you know. It's colour, colour in its full and wonderful range'; about people being refractions of light; about his colour ('brown'); about the nature and dynamic of prayer and of the Eucharist; and the Emmaus Road.

And we talked about his 'unfinished business', particularly 'the book' (this book). I told him, 'It's been amazing to me, the process of that book: how it hasn't been just you writing the book. It's been you and Peter; you and me; you and David . . . It's drawn us all into it and it's going to be an ongoing thing, and you're still going to be part of it – carrying on – just as you're still going to be caring for us and carrying on doing what you've always been doing in this life: discerning and believing and encouraging the Spirit in each one of us. And you'll still be blessing us and interceding for us.'

'I certainly will,' he said, eager and assured.

My father had glimpsed a continuity that went far deeper than the radical interruption of death – that 'deeper rhythm'[16] of things – and he had no doubt at all that he would be carrying on blessing us just as he already had been for so many years.

I had a new sense of urgency: 'I don't know how much longer we have left together, Dad. Would you like me to anoint you?'

'Yes I would, I'd like that very much,' he said; and (with a smile), 'I need all the help I can get!'

'I wonder what it's going to be like [dying]?' I wondered.

And he answered very calmly: 'It's just going to happen, bit by bit: it's a matter of going with it.'

From that moment I handed over my priestly role: we now needed to be simply 'father and daughter' again and be ministered to as such. We later (following the administration of the last rites) celebrated Communion together as a family and were all hugely relieved at the end when the priest said, 'Well, that's the formal goodbye – but now you hold on to him for as long as you can . . .'[17]

Later that evening, having already said goodnight to my father, I went back again: 'Just in case anything happens tonight Dad, you know how much I love you, don't you?'

He answered: 'I love you too. Double. Complete.' These were the last words he spoke to me: words of praise, just as he had hoped.

From that time on he was unable to speak, although we carried on our discourses nevertheless, pretty sure that he was still able to hear. From time to time he responded by moving his (very distinctive) eyebrows and, when it was something really important to him (such as hearing the news that my brothers were on their way), and by mustering every ounce of energy within him, with a beaming smile.[18] Radiating that 'bright mysterious core, broadening and deepening, on and on and on . . .', [19] 'the fullness of him who fills all in all'.[20]

The whole family was gathered – surrounding him with the 'ordinariness' of life and love that was also very special – and for the first time there was the sense that somehow, 'all would be well'.[21] Alone with him later, I said, 'It's OK, Dad; we're going to be all right. You can let go when you need to.'

We read a favourite poem together:

In Crosslight Now

In crosslight now all faces of my friends.
Every minute still so full, so precious,
A furious intensity of knowing it ends.

That everything happened just as it has,
A variation expanding the glory of a theme;
That I bear the mystery of my mistress jazz.

To fill with gratitude, even to soar.
That one swallow that shall not fall.
A caring less which means my caring more.

Each small gesture, every utterance,
The glances I hoard. Some love is mine,
And always mine. A peace. A radiance

I've wanted to word but can't. My part
My own variation shaping this history
Of a theme as though one narrow heart

Contains the fractured voices of humanity.
Rhythms chosen, riffs of light and dark.
Autumn seems so steeped in her eternity.

Micheal O'Siadhail[22]

That night I dreamed: 'I am with Dad in the Oncology clinic at Addenbrooke's. I am critically ill and am going to die and so is Dad. It's not dreadful; it's just going to happen.'

I woke early the next morning and went in to relieve the nurse, who had been keeping watch with him. I looked at my dear father, as he lay 'bubbling', working hard for each breath, amazed at how helpless and vulnerable he had become: like a child labouring to be born and having to make the transition out of his own body. It was too hard: 'Babies die when labour goes on too long – this is longer than any labour!' I groaned. 'It's too long: it's too hard for him, God, his dying will kill him! Help him!'

And his breathing suddenly changed and then stopped as he 'gave up his spirit' as dawn broke and the sun began to rise, streaming in on him, as we said our goodbyes.

Several months later, a Muslim friend of my father's told me of a dream she had had after learning of his death:

I am in a place I've never been before: it's a strange and beautiful place. There is gold everywhere: a bit like fine dust or sand, but it's not sand – it's gold, glistening gold. It's very bright: usually I'm a person who can't stand bright light, but here in this light I can open my eyes wide. As I look up and around in the sky, I can see Dan's face smiling at me – everywhere – and all around. And he's speaking to me: not with his voice or in words but communicating to me deep in my heart and it's about God. I realize that in my hands there is a scroll, and Dan is telling me to read it: I know that it's about God. Then I'm back in normality again and I have a deep sense of peace and wellbeing.[23]

'Were you not disappointed to be back in "normality" again?' I asked.

'Not at all,' she replied. 'Dan has reassured and affirmed me and I feel much stronger and more confident for it.'

They said to each other, 'Were not our hearts burning within us while he was talking to us on the road, while he was opening the scriptures to us?'[24]

Notes

1 The more 'theoretical' part of the book, as it was conceived at the time (as he had told it to Peter): at that time it was thought that Peter might be the sole editor of this book, as it was conceived then.

2 Micheal O'Siadhail, 'In Crosslight Now', in *Our Double Time*, Newcastle upon Tyne: Bloodaxe Books, 1998, p. 94.

3 The title of Micheal O'Siadhail's chapter in my father's Festschrift, *Essentials of Christian Community,* eds. David Ford and Denis Stamps, Edinburgh: T and T Clark, 1996.

4 He said this in conversation with David.

5 Micheal O'Siadhail, 'Apprentice', in *Our Double Time*, p. 76.

6 Micheal O'Siadhail, 'In Crosslight Now', in *Our Double Time*, p. 94

7 'You and Jen are my reality checks.' (Jen is his other daughter.)

8 'We are treated as imposters, and yet are true; as unknown, and yet are well known; as dying – and see, we are alive . . . as sorrowful, yet always rejoicing; as poor, yet making many rich; as having nothing, and yet possessing everything' (2 Cor. 6.8–10).

9 2 Corinthians 4.

10 Etty Hillesum, *An Interrupted Life and Letters and Papers from Westerbork*, New York: Henry Holt and Company, Inc., 1996, pp. 198, 225, 332.

11 On the day of his surgery, my father celebrated his last public Eucharist at the daily 8 a.m. service in St Benet's, Cambridge, when this was the gospel reading for the day.

12 Hillesum, *Interrupted Life*, p. 315.

13 The 'Daniel' in the dream appeared as our son Daniel, who is named after my father.

14 The first time I have ever had this privilege, despite having accompanied many, many people (in a variety of relationships and roles) through their dying.

15 Daniel Hardy, 'Thoughts on a lifetime so far' (28 February 2002), a paper given at a home seminar in Cambridge.

16 Etty Hillesum: 'I have been terribly tired for days, but that, too, will pass; things come and go in a deeper rhythm and people must be taught to listen to it: it is the most important thing we have to learn in this life' (*Interrupted Life*, p. 332).

17 Gregory Seach, then one of my David's graduate students, now Dean of Clare College, Cambridge, and who presided at my father's funeral.

18 Especially, when I told him I was going to tell my brothers about our conversations together.

19 Words he used when reflecting on another of Micheal's poems, 'Autumn Report': 'Even in this fall, wholehearted life reverberates some almighty gaiety, invites me to adore the immense integrity . . . I've never felt so near the centre of all that is . . . Why hedge our bets or play too cool; detached we might miss the passion to broaden the bore, deepen the joy' (Micheal O'Siadhail, 'Autumn Report', in *Poems 1975–1995*, Newcastle upon Tyne: Bloodaxe Books, 1992, 1995, 1999, p. 83).

20 Ephesians 1.23.

21 In the sense of Mother Julian of Norwich, 'All shall be well and all shall be well and all manner of things shall be well' (*Revelations of Divine Love*, New York: Penguin Books Ltd, 1995).

22 O'Siadhail, *Our Double Time*, p. 94.

23 Dr Yamina Mermer (Muslim SR colleague and friend).

24 Luke 24.32.

Daniel W. Hardy

9 November 1930 – 15 November 2007

'May he rest in peace and rise in glory.'
(A Christian prayer)

'*Zikhrono l'brakhah*: May His Memory Be for a Blessing'
(A Jewish prayer)

'In the Name of the Compassionate, the Kind:
to God we belong, to Him we return.' Amin
(A Muslim prayer)

Bibliography: Daniel W. Hardy

1963

'The Doctrine of Sin: An Investigation of the Theories of Karl Barth and F. R. Tennant' (Thesis, General Theological Seminary, New York, 1963).

1966

'Anglican Theology' ('La Théologie Anglicane', Université de Lyon, 1966).

1967

'The Method of Duality in Theology' (University of Birmingham, 1967).
'What Framework for Theology?', *Regina* (Birmingham; The Queen's College, 1967).

1968

'Language and Theology' (Thesis, Oxford University, 1968).

1969

'Anxiety in Theological Perspective' (Institute of Religion and Medicine, Birmingham, 1969).

1970

'What Does It Mean to Love?', *Theology* 73 (1970), pp. 257–64.

1971

'The Methods of Knowledge in 17th and 18th Century Theology' (University of Birmingham, 1971).
'A Taxonomy of Theologies' (University of Birmingham, 1971).

1972

'Reality and Its Realization in Theology' (University of Birmingham, 1972).
'The Study of Theology' (University of Birmingham, 1972).

1973

'Christian Theology as Realism' (University of Birmingham, 1973).

'The Ordination of Women to the Priesthood' (Birmingham Diocesan Synod, 1973).

1974

'The Church in Change', in *Structures for Ministry*, the first report of the Needs and Resources Commission Diocese of Birmingham (Birmingham: Church House, 1974).

'Completeness and Change in Christian Doctrine' (University of Birmingham, 1974).

'The Ideal of Integration in 17th and 18th Century Theology' (University of Birmingham, 1974).

'Theology and the Effect of the European Enlightenment' (University of Birmingham, 1974).

1975

'Teaching Religion: A Theological Critique', *Learning for Living* 15/1 (1975), pp. 257–64.

'Unity and Duality as Theological Ideals' (University of Birmingham, 1975).

'The Use of Information-Theory in Theology' (American Academy of Religion, 1975).

With Alan Bryman and J. G. Davies, *In-Service Training for Clergy* (Birmingham: Institute of Worship and Architecture, 1975).

1977

'The Implications of Pluralism for Religious Education', *Learning for Living* 17/2 (1977), pp. 55–62.

'Man the Creature', *Scottish Journal of Theology* 30/2 (1977), pp. 111–36.

'Theology and the Academic World' (University of Birmingham, 1977).

1978

'Coleridge and Hegel' (University of Birmingham, 1978).

'Coleridge's Hunger for Eternity' (American Academy of Religion, 1978).

'Truth in Religious Education: Further Reflections on the Implications of Pluralism', *British Journal of Religious Education* 1/3 (1978), pp. 102–7; republished in John Hull, ed., *New Directions in Religious Education* (Lewes: The Falmer Press, 1982).

1979

'Christianity as the Foundation of Moral Life' (University of Birmingham, 1979).

'Guidelines in Current Theology', *The Bishopric* [Church House, Birmingham] 1/3 (1979), pp. 4–8.

'The Training of Lay Readers' (Diocese of Birmingham, 1979).

BIBLIOGRAPHY

1980

'The Black Manifesto' (University of Birmingham, 1980).

'Christian Affirmation and the Structure of Personal Life', in Thomas F. Torrance, ed., *Belief in Science and Christian Life: The Relevance of Michael Polanyi's Thought for Christian Faith and Life* (Edinburgh: The Handsel Press, 1980), pp. 71–90.

'Natural Science and Christian Theology', *King's College Review* [King's College, London] 3/2 (1980), pp. 41–9.

'Realization Theory', 'Relativism', 'Operationalism' and 'Subjectivism' in *Theology*, and 'Openness to the World and to God'; interfaculty lectures (University of Birmingham, 1980).

1981

'Christ and Creation', in Thomas F. Torrance, ed., *The Incarnation: Ecumenical Studies in the Nicene-Constantinopolitan Creed A. D. 381* (Edinburgh: The Handsel Press, 1981), pp. 88–110.

'The Study of Theology in Universities' (University of Leeds, 1981).

'Today's Word for Today: Gerhard Ebeling', *Expository Times* 93/3 (1981), pp. 68–72.

1982

'Religion and Social Righteousness' (University of Birmingham, 1982).

1983

'The Dynamics of Creation' (Society for the Study of Theology, 1983).

1984

'Integrating Training for Theology Graduates' (Advisory Council for the Church's Ministry, London, 1984).

'Pastoral Studies: An Interdisciplinary Activity' (Anniversary Conference, University of Birmingham, 1984).

'Why Special Training for Black Clergy?' (Advisory Council for the Church's Ministry, London, 1984).

With David F. Ford, *Jubilate: Theology in Praise* (London: Darton, Longman & Todd, 1984); published in the USA as *Praising and Knowing God* (Philadelphia: Westminster, 1985).

1985

Education for the Church's Ministry (London: Advisory Council for the Church's Ministry, 1985).

'The Nineteenth Century in Britain: Coleridge, the Agnostics and the Idealists', in *Papers of the Nineteenth Century Theology Working Group*, Vol. 13, American Academy of Religion, 1985.

'Religious Education: Truth Claims or Meaning-Giving?', in Marius Felderhof, ed., *Religious Education in a Pluralistic Society* (London: Hodder & Stoughton, 1985), pp. 101–15.

1986

'The Repossession of the Church in Birmingham', *The Bishopric* [Church House, Birmingham] 8/2 (1986), pp. 9–19.

'Thanksgiving (USA)', in J. G. Davies, ed., *A New Dictionary of Liturgy and Worship* (London: SCM; Philadelphia: Westminster, 1986), pp. 504–5.

1987

'Coleridge on the Trinity', *Anglican Theological Review* 69 (April 1987), pp. 145–55.

1988

'The English Tradition of Interpretation and the Reception of Schleiermacher and Barth in England', in James O. Duke and Robert F. Streetman, eds, *Barth and Schleiermacher: Beyond the Impasse?* (Philadelphia: Fortress Press, 1988), pp. 138–61.

'Rationality, the Sciences and Theology', in Geoffrey Wainwright, ed., *Keeping the Faith: Essays to Mark the Centenary of Lux Mundi* (Philadelphia: Fortress Press / London: SPCK, 1988), pp. 274–309.

'Truth and the Election of God's People' (Carlisle Cathedral, 1988).

1989

'British Theologians: Theology through Philosophy', in David F. Ford, ed., *The Modern Theologians: An Introduction*, Vol. 2 (Oxford: Blackwell, 1989), pp. 30–71.

'Church, Ministry and Sacraments: Fourteen Lectures' (University of Durham, 1989).

'Created and Redeemed Sociality', in Colin E. Gunton and Daniel W. Hardy, eds, *On Being the Church: Essays on the Christian Community* (Edinburgh: T & T Clark, 1989), pp. 21–47.

'Introduction to Theology: Eight Lectures' (University of Durham, 1989).

'The Nature of a University' (University of Durham, 1989).

'On Leadership and Priesthood' (University of Newcastle, 1989).

'Spirit of Unity – Reconcile Your People' (Commission on Faith and Order, World Council of Churches, Würzburg, Germany, 1989).

'Thomas F. Torrance', in David F. Ford, ed., *The Modern Theologians: An Introduction*, Vol. 1 (Oxford: Blackwell, 1989), pp. 71–91.

1990

'The Doctrine of Creation in 19th Century Theology: A Preface to Discussion', in *Papers of the Nineteenth Century Theology Group*, Vol. 16, American Academy of Religion, 1990.

'Systematic Theology', in J. L. Houlden, ed., *Dictionary of Biblical Interpretation* (London: SCM / Philadelphia: TPI, 1990), pp. 665–7.

'The Value of Land' (Newcastle City Chaplaincy, 1990).

BIBLIOGRAPHY

1991

The Center's Identity and Future Program: The Director's Report for 1991 (Princeton: Center of Theological Inquiry, 1991).

'Epilogue: The Strategy of Liberalism', in Daniel W. Hardy and Peter H. Sedgwick, eds, *The Weight of Glory: A Vision and Practice for Christian Theology. The Future of Liberal Theology: Essays for Peter Baelz* (Edinburgh: T & T Clark, 1991), pp. 299–306.

'The Foundation of Cognition and Ethics in Worship' (Durham–Tübingen Consultation, 1991).

The Future of the Center of Theological Inquiry (Princeton: Center of Theological Inquiry, 1991).

'God and the Form of Society', in Daniel W. Hardy and Peter H. Sedgwick, eds, *The Weight of Glory: A Vision and Practice for Christian Theology. The Future of Liberal Theology: Essays for Peter Baelz* (Edinburgh: T & T Clark, 1991), pp. 131–44.

'On the Ordination of Homosexuals' (Episcopal Church General Convention, 1991).

Planning for the Future of the Center (Princeton: Center of Theological Inquiry, 1991).

'The Recovery of Christian Faith in Modern Life' (Church of St Michael & St George, St Louis, 1991).

'The Religion of America' (Trinity Church, Princeton, 1991).

'On the Public Character of Theology' (Higher Education Chaplains' Conference, High Leigh, 1991).

'The Search for Order and Dynamism in Anglicanism' (Trinity Church, Princeton, 1991).

'Theological Inquiry Today' (Old Guards' Association, Princeton, 1991).

'Theology and Life's Irreducible Structure' (Polanyi Centenary, St. George's House, Windsor, 1991).

1992

'The Debate about the Ordination of Women' (London, 1992).

'Developing Christian Faith for the 21st Century' (St Barnabas Church, Greenwich, 1992).

'The Relationship of the Mainline Churches and Fundamentalism' (Trinity Church, Princeton, 1992).

'Sociality, Rationality and Culture: Faith Embedded in the Particularities of History', in *Papers of the Nineteenth Century Theology Working Group*, Vol. 18, American Academy of Religion, 1992.

'The Trinity in Language' (Annual Lecture, Scholars Engaged in Anglican Doctrine, Alexandria, 1992).

'Where Is Home? Identity and Diaspora in Christianity' (Consultation on Inter Religious Relations, Center of Theological Inquiry, Princeton, 1992).

'Worship as the Orientation of Life to God', *Ex Auditu* 8 (1992), pp. 55–71.

1993

'The Center of Theological Inquiry: History and Future' (Nassau Club, Princeton, 1993).

'The Future of the Church' (St Barnabas Church, Greenwich, 1993).

'The Future of the Church: An Exploration' (Princeton, 1993).

'The Future of Theology in a Complex World', in Hilary D. Regan and Alan J. Torrance, eds, *Christ and Context: The Confrontation between Gospel and Culture* (Edinburgh: T & T Clark, 1993), pp. 21–42.

'Sin and Confession' (All Saints' Church, Princeton, 1993).

'The Spirit of God in Creation and Reconciliation', in Hilary D. Regan and Alan J. Torrance, eds, *Christ and Context: The Confrontation between Gospel and Culture* (Edinburgh: T & T Clark, 1993), pp. 237–58.

'Theology, Cosmology and Change' (Society for the Study of Theology, 1993).

An Unfolding Strategy: The Director's Report for 1992 (Princeton: Center of Theological Inquiry, 1993).

1994

'Dimensions of Interfaith Dialogue' (Consulate General of India, New York, 1994).

The Nature of Theological Inquiry: The Director's Report for 1993 (Princeton: Center of Theological Inquiry, 1994).

'The Orientation of Life to God' (Princeton, 1994).

'The Question of God in "God's Action in the World"' (Consultation on Theology and Science, CTI, Princeton, 1994).

'The Situation of Christian Faith Today and a Response' (New York, 1994).

1995

'Covenant', 'Creation', and 'Worship', in Paul A. B. Clarke and Andrew Linzey, eds, *The Dictionary of Theology and Society* (London: Routledge & Kegan Paul, 1995).

The Logic of Interdisciplinary Studies and the Coherence of Theology: The Director's Report for 1994 (Princeton: Center of Theological Inquiry, 1995).

'The Roots of Values' (Old Guards' Association, Princeton, 1995).

1996

'Creation and Eschatology', in Colin E. Gunton, ed., *The Doctrine of Creation* (London: SPCK, 1996).

'God in the Ordinary: The Work of J. G. Davies (1919–1990)', *Theology* 99/792 (1996), pp. 427–40.

God's Ways with the World: Thinking and Practising Christian Faith (Edinburgh: T & T Clark, 1996).

'A Magnificent Complexity: Letting God be God in Church, Society and Creation', in David F. Ford and Dennis Stamps, eds, *Essentials of Christian Community: For Daniel W. Hardy on His 65th Birthday* (Edinburgh: T & T Clark, 1996), pp. 307–56.

'Theology and the Cultural Reduction of Religion', in J. Astley and L.

Francis, eds, *Christian Theology and Religious Education: Connections and Contradictions* (London: SPCK, 1996), pp. 16–32.

1998

'Spirituality and its Embodiment in Church Life', in Eric O. Springsted, ed., *Spirituality and Theology: Essays in Honor of Diogenes Allen* (Louisville, KY: Westminster/John Knox Press, 1998), pp. 133–47.

1999

'Calvinism and the Visual Arts: A Theological Introduction', in Paul Corby Finney, ed., *Seeing Beyond the Word: Visual Arts and Calvinist Tradition* (Grand Rapids: Eerdmans, 1999), pp. 1–16.

'Gerald Bonner: An Appreciation', in Robert Dodaro and George Lawless, eds, *Augustine and His Critics* (London: Routledge, 1999), pp. 5–10.

'The Grace of God and Earthly Wisdom', in Stephen Barton, ed., *Where Shall Wisdom Be Found* (Edinburgh: T & T Clark, 1999), pp. 231–47.

'Reasoning after Revelation: Dialogues in Postmodern Jewish Philosophy', *Modern Theology* 15/4 (1999), pp. 519–20.

2000

'Eschatology as a Challenge for Theology', in David Fergusson and Marcel Sarot, eds, *The Future as God's Gift: Essays in Christian Eschatology* (Edinburgh: T & T Clark, 2000), pp. 151–8.

2001

'Birmingham Days', *Religion* 31/4 (2001), pp. 331–2.

Finding the Church: The Dynamic Truth of Anglicanism (London: SCM Press, 2001).

'Upholding Orthodoxy in Missionary Encounters: A Theological Perspective', in Brian Stanley, ed., *Christian Missions and the Enlightenment* (Grand Rapids: Eerdmans, 2001), pp. 198–222.

2002

'Abraham's Visitors', *The Journal of Scriptural Reasoning* (electronic) 2/3 (September 2002).

'Pharaoh's Hardened Heart', *The Journal of Scriptural Reasoning* (electronic) 2/2 (September 2002).

'A Response to the Consultation', in Thomas F. Foust, ed., *Scandalous Prophet: The Way of Mission after Newbigin* (Grand Rapids: Eerdmans, 2002), pp. 227–33.

'The Rules of Scriptural Reasoning', *The Journal of Scriptural Reasoning* (electronic) 2/1 (May 2002).

'Textual Reasoning: A Concluding Reflection', in P. Ochs and N. Levene, eds, *Textual Reasonings: Jewish Philosophy and Text Study at the end of the Twentieth Century* (London: SCM Press, 2002; and Grand Rapids, MI: Eerdmans, 2003), pp. 269–76.

2003

'The Promise of Trinitarian Theology: Theologians in Dialogue with T. F. Torrance', *Theology* 106/833 (2003), pp. 368–9.

'The Song of Songs', *The Journal of Scriptural Reasoning* (electronic) 3/2 (August 2003).

'Worship and the Formation of a Holy People', in Stephen Barton, ed., *Holiness Past and Present* (London: T & T Clark, 2003), pp. 477–98.

2004

'Image of God: Scriptural Anthropology: A Response to the Papers', *The Journal of Scriptural Reasoning* (electronic) 4/2 (October 2004).

2005

'Karl Barth', in David F. Ford and Rachel Muers, eds, *The Modern Theologians*, third edn (Malden, MA: Blackwell, 2005), pp. 21–42.

'Societal Economics and the Kingdom of God: A Consideration of Two Parables of the Kingdom (Matthew 18.21–35 and 20.1–16)', *The Journal of Scriptural Reasoning* (electronic) 5/2 (August 2005).

'T. F. Torrance', in David F. Ford and Rachel Muers, eds, *The Modern Theologians*, third edn (Malden, MA: Blackwell, 2005), pp. 163–77.

With David F. Ford, *Living in Praise: Worshipping and Knowing God* (Grand Rapids: Baker Academic, 2005).

2006

'Harmony and Mutual Implication in the Opus Maximum', in Jeffrey W. Barbeau, ed., *Coleridge's Assertion of Religion: Essays on the Opus Maximum*, Leuven, Paris, Dudley, MA: Peeters, 2006, pp. 33–52.

'John Macquarrie's Ecclesiology', in Robert Morgan, ed., *In Search of Humanity and Deity: A Celebration of John Macquarrie's Theology* (London: SCM Press, 2006), pp. 267–76.

'The Promise of Scriptural Reasoning', *Modern Theology* 22/3 (2006), pp. 529–51; and in D. Ford and C. Pecknold, eds, *The Promise of Scriptural Reasoning* (Oxford: Blackwell, 2006), pp. 185–207.

2008

'Receptive Ecumenism: Learning by Engagement', in Paul D. Murray, ed., *Receptive Ecumenism and the Call to Catholic Learning: Exploring a Way for Contemporary Ecumenism* (Oxford: Oxford University Press, 2008), pp. 428–41.

'Theology and Spirituality: A Tribute to Ann Loades', in Natalie K. Watson and Stephen Burns, eds, *Exchanges of Grace: Essays in Honour of Ann Loades* (London: SCM Press, 2008), pp. 103–19.

'The Trial of the Witnesses: The Rise and Decline of Postliberal Theology', *Theology* 111/860 (2008), pp. 127–8.

Index

Biblical References